because God has called

devotions for
church workers

tom rogers

CPH®
SAINT LOUIS

In memory of Helen Naomi Christopher, my
hero in the faith and my grandma

Contents

~1~

Why Am I Here?

> From one man He made every nation of men, that
> they should inhabit the whole earth; and He deter-
> mined the times set for them and the exact places
> where they should live. God did this so that men
> would seek Him and perhaps reach out for Him and
> find Him, though He is not far from each one of us.
> *Acts 17:26–27*

At the end of a difficult day, a church worker thought, "Why am I here? I'm constantly away from my home and family. I give and give and give, but no one seems to appreciate what I'm doing. The kids I work with don't respect me, much less like me, and the adults I work with disregard me. I seem to be getting nowhere fast. Why am I here?"

Mother Theresa of Calcutta was asked what it was about Calcutta that had caused her to spend her entire life there. Her response? "I'm not in Calcutta because I love it. I'm in Calcutta because God called me to be here."

The passage from Acts shares a similar thought with church workers. You are here because God called you to be here. It may seem like you are here because of a placement process or because an acquaintance knew that a church was looking for a worker. It may seem that you are here because of a completely human act. That's not the case. The God who has "determined the times set for them and the exact places where they should live" placed you right where you can best serve His kingdom. God put you here, as Luke says, so people "would seek Him and perhaps reach out for Him and find Him."

Only the devil benefits from church workers who feel unfit for service where God has placed them. God would have us take comfort in the fact that where we serve is part of His plan. God is seeking people who live where you serve. He wants them to know the same Good News of salvation that You have to share. He knows that the Holy Spirit can use you and the Word with which He has equipped you to reach them. What a great reason to be here!

The Prayer: O Lord, I know that You have placed me here for service. Help me resist the devil's temptation to believe I'm in the wrong place. Allow me to see and rejoice in the fruit that You are causing me to bear right here. In Jesus' name. Amen.

~2~

Taking My Medicine

To the Jews who had believed Him, Jesus said, "If you hold to My teaching, you are really My disciples. Then you will know the truth, and the truth will set you free." *John 8:31–32*

My physician was very clear. I had a disease. The "silent killer," she called it. She told me not to despair; I can have a long and fruitful life, if I take the medicine she prescribed. I do. For me, it is a matter of life and death. My physician made it clear: My condition means that without medication, I could die.

Jesus is clear as well. "If you continue in My teaching, you are really My disciples. Then you will know the truth, and the truth will set you free." Jesus reminds us that we carry a deadly disease called sin. Sin does not literally make us drop dead from a stroke or heart attack, but it does make us selfish, difficult, loveless, and discouraging. That's why Jesus encourages us to continue in His Word and to do so just as faithfully as we take life-saving medication. His Word is the only place we find forgiveness and eternal healing.

"I can't take the time" is a popular reason for not studying the Word daily. Perhaps we believe that we need to devote long, hard hours to such study to receive the benefit Jesus has prepared for us. This isn't true. Devotions that make us strong for Christian life and service are not helpful because of their length. Instead, their strength comes from Scripture.

It didn't take long for God to say, "Let there be light," but history was forever changed because of those words. It doesn't take long to read phrases such as, "The Lord is my shepherd"; "I will be with you always"; and "Speak the truth in love." But those phrases, through the work of the Holy Spirit, accomplish in us that for which God sent them. No one needs to dedicate a long period of time for personal devotions. If you have the time, it's wonderful; God will bless its use. If you don't have the time, don't despair. Put your Bible next to your medicine cabinet, take your medication, read your Bible sentence, and meditate on that passage all day long. Trust that God will make you healthy in mind, body, and spirit.

The Prayer: Lord, Your Word is my strength, but I often believe I don't have time to devote to Your Word. Thank You for reminding me that even a glimpse at Your Word can fill me with light and power. Keep me faithful to the study of Your Word, O Lord, and thank You for the life and health it gives. In Jesus' name. Amen.

Christ in the Critic

Brothers, if someone is caught in a sin, you who are spiritual should restore him gently. *Galatians 6:1*

"It was Memorial Day and we didn't sing any patriotic hymns, Pastor. Isn't anybody a patriot anymore?"

"You can say what you want, Pastor, but I don't think you know how the changes you're bringing about are upsetting our people."

"Pastor, I don't like the direction your preaching has taken in the last few weeks. All that talk about money upsets me. And I'm not the only one. There are a lot of us who will leave the church if this doesn't stop."

Criticism happens. It even happened to Jesus. St. Paul records in 2 Corinthians 5:16: "So from now on we regard no one from a worldly point of view. Though we once regarded Christ in this way, we do so no longer." Jesus was called everything from a drunkard and a glutton to a follower of Beelzebub. Servants certainly are not above their master, so servants of Christ will receive the same thing. Being criticized is not the issue; the issue is what to do when it happens.

Paul offers both counsel and comfort. In Galatians, he clearly indicates to whom we should listen. If our critic has the reputation of one who is "spiritual" and approaches us in a spirit of "gentleness," then we have reason to believe this person is a messenger from the Lord. Such people have no desire to hurt our feelings. Instead, they recognize the legitimacy of our ministry and want to point out a behavior or attitude that compromises it. We can listen to these critics and thank them. They are supporters. They risk engaging our anger to improve our ability to serve in accordance with Christ's wishes.

Then there are those critics who want to hurt our feelings and put us in our place. In these people, gentleness is replaced by accusations and threats. They speak as representatives of the voice of opposition. When these people approach us, Jesus gives us an opportunity to sow the seed of love in an angry person's soul, just as He sowed that seed when we opposed Him. With these critics, we pray that the Holy Spirit would give us an overwhelming love for them. We pray that our speech would be gracious and seasoned with salt. We ask Him to open our ears to really listen. If their concerns are valid, we honor them by considering them. If their concerns are not valid, we lovingly tell them so and express our sorrow that they feel this way. Instead of winning an argument, we may win a person to a life guided by the love of Christ.

Still, Jesus tells us in Matthew 10 that there will be those who will never receive us or our message. In these cases, Jesus encourages us not to let these people keep us awake at night; instead, we are to move on in our ministry.

We thank God that in a vocation where criticism happens, we can take our concerns to the Lord. He knows what criticism feels like. He has the power to get us through those times and restore the joy of our ministry.

The Prayer: Lord Jesus, You understand the pain of criticism. Give me Your wisdom to know which critics are speaking for You and which are speaking for the opposition. Help me to accept criticism that builds up Your kingdom and ignore criticism that opposes Your will. At all times, fill me with Your love for my critics. In Your name. Amen.

~4~

Letting Go of Our Egos

For by the grace given me I say to every one of you: Do
not think of yourself more highly than you ought, but
rather think of yourself with sober judgment, in accordance with the measure of faith God has given you.
Romans 12:3

My ego had become addicted to the words of the worshipers as they funneled out of church. "Great sermon,
Pastor." "That one really spoke to me today, Reverend." I
believed these supporters. I was a good preacher. At least that
was one area of ministry where I could excel.

One day, a retired minister stopped on his way out of
church. "You are a fairly good preacher," he said, "but you
could be better if you would separate yourself from your
manuscript. Spend more time getting familiar with your sermon so you don't need to take the manuscript into the pulpit. I'll be here to measure your progress."

I was crushed. He had found shortcomings in the one
area of my profession where I felt I did a good job. I felt like
resigning. My hurt quickly turned into defensive anger.
"Who does that old fossil think he's talking to? He hasn't
been in a pulpit for so long, he couldn't find his way there
with the church lights on. How dare he criticize me?"

I fumed over this for several weeks. Each Sunday the
pulpit was uncomfortable. I felt like I was under a micro-
scope. Then I wandered across these words of St. Paul: "Do
not think of yourself more highly than you ought." I had
surely done that. Contrition fell over my heart, but I also
knew the certainty of God's forgiveness. Maybe the old

preacher was right. Yes, it will require a lot more work, but if it will help people and offer a better way to serve Jesus …

As I implemented this new style, there were a few embarrassing moments when my mind went blank. I had to ask the congregation for patience while I mastered this technique. But sooner than expected, I began preaching manuscript-free. I maintained eye contact. People commented on how easy it was to listen now that I was "talking to them"!

That preacher was a messenger of God who wanted to make me more effective. All he had to do was talk to me. God had His work cut out for Him, though! God had to break down my ego. The thing that makes sin what it is, they say, is the "I" in the middle. They are right.

When Jesus counted equality with God not as something to be grasped but emptied Himself, taking on the form of a servant and becoming obedient, even to death on a cross (paraphrase of Philippians 2:6ff), He established a model for us—a model, when emulated, that helps others see Jesus.

Does your ego cling to some part of your ministry? Is it an administrative style? An unyielding homework policy? An overly stringent discipline policy? An insistence that your family should understand your absenteeism because you work for the Lord? Stop and repeat these words of Paul: "Do not think of yourself more highly than you ought, but rather think of yourself with sober judgment." Then watch how the Holy Spirit will make you the servant He wants you to be. If that's hard, pray that God sends a retired preacher, teacher, deaconess, or DCE to bring you to your Christ-centered senses.

The Prayer: Lord, You know the size of my ego. You know that my ego can compromise the effectiveness of my ministry. Lord, by Your grace, pare away at my ego. In Your Holy name. Amen.

Why Worry?

Do not be anxious about anything, but in everything, by prayer and petition, with thanksgiving, present your requests to God. And the peace of God, which transcends all understanding, will guard your hearts and your minds in Christ Jesus. *Philippians 4:6–7*

The professional golfer Lee Trevino grew up in an impoverished neighborhood. He joined the army and discovered that he had the ability to play golf well. He was so good that he supplemented his army pay by wagering with affluent officers on the golf course.

In every sense of the word, Lee Trevino was a hustler. He took huge risks. Sometimes he would bet sums of money so large he never could have covered them if he lost. He depended only on his skill to keep him out of trouble.

When he turned professional, Trevino again found himself playing for large sums of money. At one tournament, a single putt was worth $200,000. He made it. A reporter asked Trevino what the pressure was like while putting for $200,000. Trevino replied, "There is no pressure in putting for $200,000 of someone else's money. When you're putting for $20 and know you only have $5 in your pocket, now that's pressure."

When it comes to worry and anxiety among church workers, it may appear as though we believe we have only $5 in our pocket and no confidence that we can make the putt. The list of things about which we may be anxious includes pleasing the church's leaders, the school's parents, or our colleagues; getting too far behind in our work; and neglecting our families or health. To all of this, God says, "Be still, and know that I am God" (Psalm 46:10).

It may sound naive to the contemporary mind, but whatever troubles us, God determined a solution to the problem even before the world began. Scripture bears witness to this truth on every page. Joshua questioned his ability to follow in Moses' sandals. God took care of that. Joseph worried about what to do when he discovered that Mary was "with child." God took care of that. Mary worried about what would happen to her friends if anyone discovered that the wine was gone. Jesus took care of that. The disciples wondered how they would feed all those people with a few loaves of bread and a couple of fish. Jesus took care of that. The women on the way to the tomb that first Easter morning worried about who would remove the stone. Jesus took care of that.

God really is in control of our lives. Jesus' resurrection proves it. We are capable of missing any "putt," even the short ones, but God can use our mistakes to His glory. He doesn't promise us a rose garden, but we always can rely on His love and strength to comfort us when the chips are down. Just ask Moses, David, Peter, and Paul about that.

For those of us who refuse comfort, consider this: If we must worry, Jesus, who loves us so much that He died for our every sin, says, "I won't prevent you from worrying. I still love you." Even if you miss the "putt," Jesus' love supersedes your worries.

The Prayer: Dear Jesus, You have been solving people's problems for centuries. Send Your Holy Spirit into my heart to remind me again that I can be still and know that You are God. Teach me to replace worry with trust. In Jesus' name. Amen.

~ 6 ~

Grace and Peace ... to Them

Grace and peace to you from God our Father and the Lord Jesus Christ, who gave Himself for our sins to rescue us from the present evil age, according to the will of our God and Father, to whom be glory for ever and ever. Amen. *Galatians 1:3–5*

It was a mess, a big mess. Just when we thought the school year was over. Just when we had wished one another a happy summer vacation. Just when we had watched the kids sign one another's yearbooks—we saw it. "It" was in the middle of the eighth-grade class picture. One young man from our "Christian" school had made a "hidden" gesture to the camera. It was hidden through the assembly stage of the book. It was hidden to the publishers and to our faculty advisor as he reviewed the galley sheets. But two days before school was out, it was there for all to see. A horrible vulgarity had soiled the pages of our yearbook.

The discovery of this "gesture" gave occasion to one of those pastor/principal meetings that go best if the two get along well. After a brief discussion, we decided to recall the yearbooks, return them to the publisher for changes, and distribute new yearbooks to the students.

Then came the issue of the student. What should be done with him? I must admit that my first impulse was to take him to the sanctuary, show him the altar, and remind him that in many ancient cultures, children were sacrificed. Our principal agreed in principle, but such an action seemed inconsistent with our mission statement to "Communicate Christ's love to everyone everywhere and our love for Him."

It was the mission statement that got us back on track. This young man had caused us a river of grief. We received dozens of phone calls from upset parents—phone calls that began with the words, "But we thought this was a Christian school." It's a good thing for that guilty student that we are a Christian school.

Instead of consigning this malicious young man to the devil, we met with him and his parents. Before the meeting, the principal and I asked God to enable us to see that this student was His beloved child. We asked God to help us show Jesus to this young man, even as we assigned consequences for his sinful behavior.

God answered our prayers. The situation was resolved by the Spirit of God, who enables victims of sin to see sinners as beloved of God whose sins are forgiven because of Jesus' sacrifice on the cross. With the support of the parents, the issue was resolved without screaming, shouting, or name-calling.

St. Paul was disappointed by the church he had planted in Galatia. During his time in that city, people had embraced the Gospel as the Good News of salvation by grace through faith alone. They embraced the happy news that we cannot contribute to our salvation. As soon as Paul left Galatia, a group of Jewish Christians convinced the new believers that observing Jewish festivals and rituals also was necessary for salvation. When the news hit Paul, he must have felt like our school community did when we saw the yearbook. Anger, disappointment, and resentment must have run through Paul's mind and heart. But when he penned his epistle, he addressed his readers with grace and peace from God our Father and the Lord Jesus Christ.

Paul didn't forget that these erring Christians were beloved of God, still capable of change because of the Holy Spirit. As those who work in the name of Jesus, we have the same attitude. We may be at our wits' end, ready to excommunicate a person, but that desire submits to God's will and Christ's love. The only hope for this boy or the church of Galatia was to see again the love and patience of Jesus—a love and patience so sincere and powerful that it captures the heart and mind.

The incident with the young man happened years ago. He has since matured in faith. The incident with the church at Galatia happened years ago as well, and Jesus triumphed there. As professional church workers, the Holy Spirit works through us to make that triumph possible as we apply and practice God's Word.

The Prayer: Lord Jesus, You came to save sinners. Help me recall the love You have for me and all sinners. Let me treat people with grace and peace. In Your name and for Your sake. Amen.

~7~

Paul and Barnabas, John Mark and Us

> Some time later Paul said to Barnabas, "Let us go back and visit the brothers in all the towns where we preached the word of the Lord and see how they are doing." Barnabas wanted to take John, also called Mark, with them, but Paul did not think it wise to take him, because he had deserted them in Pamphylia and had not continued with them in the work. They had such a sharp disagreement that they parted company.
> *Acts 15:36–39*

A person can only speculate as to what caused Paul and Barnabas to "part company." Perhaps Paul was angry at John Mark for his lack of courage and for deserting them in Pamphylia. Perhaps Paul was intolerant of the patience that Barnabas showed toward John Mark. Maybe Paul was dissatisfied with their level of willingness to minister to the Gentiles. We do know that something caused enough commotion to break up the missionary team.

Sometimes it's that way with problems among modern church workers. We may not know what has upset them, but before we know it, they have separated.

One thing we do know about Paul, Barnabas, and John Mark: Whatever the problem, God took both sides. Paul took Silas and continued to work in Syria and Cilicia. The Bible says that they strengthened the churches. John Mark and Barnabas went wherever the Lord sent them and also strengthened and extended the Church. God finds productive and positive ways to bypass human disputes.

Although God works according to His holy will, we may consider separation from others to make a point. And separation doesn't always mean a physical distance. Sometimes team members stop talking to each other or talk with third parties about a conflict. The devil helps us believe that our ideas, feelings, and opinions are priceless. Jesus, who is the head of the Church, will not allow such conflict to stop His work. And as the one who reconciled us with God, He offers the power of reconciliation to those in conflict.

It must grieve God when His workers can't work, speak, pray, or worship together. Jesus, who died for the forgiveness of sins, refuses to let petty problems obstruct the Church's ministry. He may bless both sides of an argument or dispute. By doing this, Jesus focuses our attention on what is truly important. And what is truly important is not our "correctness," but His mission—spreading the Good News.

For Paul and Barnabas, the Good News went out; in fact, the proclamation was multiplied. Not only did the Church grow, but Barnabas, Paul, and John Mark were reconciled. Paul even called John Mark a beloved son.

At times, church workers will divide over issues that seem significant at the time. But Jesus knows better. God always blesses the work of people who serve according to His will. Therefore, there are few good reasons to separate. Instead, we trust the power of the Holy Spirit to reconcile us through Jesus Christ. When Jesus made us one with Himself, He also made it possible for all Christians to be one.

The Prayer: Lord, help me avoid ungodly division. Instead, help me see how You bless the ministry of those who raise Your name high before the world. Teach me to love those I work with and to cooperate with them according to Your will. In Your name. Amen.

~8~

Hope for the Discouraged

So the other disciples told [Thomas], "We have seen the Lord!" But he said to them, "Unless I see the nail marks in His hands and put my finger where the nails were, and put my hand into His side, I will not believe it." *John 20:25*

I believe that Thomas has been unfairly labeled. When you hear his name, you immediately think "doubter." I believe other Bible passages refer to Thomas in another light. John 11:16 records the disciples' fear that the opposition will kill Jesus if He visits the grave of His friend, Lazarus. Thomas alone declares, "Let us also go, that we may die with Him." That's faithful and courageous language.

In John 14:1–5, Jesus tells the disciples they shouldn't worry because He will go and prepare a place for them. He concludes those verses by saying, "You know the way to the place where I am going." The disciples have no idea what Jesus means, but Thomas is the only one with the courage to ask what might be considered a "dumb" question. "Lord, we don't know where You are going, so how can we know the way?" he queries. That's honesty mixed with trust.

I see Thomas as a person committed to Jesus and the Gospel. He's willing to die for Jesus, but he seems surprised that Jesus would die for him. Thomas' faith falters as he trusts himself more than his Savior. At times, Thomas, like us, doubts the Savior's role. But the label "doubter" should stick with him no more than it sticks with us. By the grace of God, faith, in any quantity, saves. Forgiveness earned by Jesus forgives even doubt. Thomas was saved not because he was bold, but because Jesus overcame timidity and weakness with compassion and forgiveness.

As church workers, we know the power of doubt. When we experience major disappointments—such as the rejection of a building program, resistance to a new form of worship, or the cutting of a school budget—we become doubters of God's power. We even may want to see a few "nail holes" ourselves—proof of God's power for our good.

Disappointed and doubting church workers receive help and hope as they read Thomas' story. Jesus doesn't come to see him just because he doubts, He comes back to comfort and assure Thomas despite his disappointment. Jesus comes to the aid of everyone whose hearts are breaking because they believe they're lost—even us. Just as He did with the disappointed Thomas, Jesus invites us to put our fingers into His hands and side through the Word and the Sacraments. Just as this act reassured Thomas that, in Jesus, he was not lost, so our recollection of this event assures us we are not lost. If wounds that once brought death now stand as witness to life, then it's a matter of time until Jesus brings us into eternity with Himself.

The Prayer: Lord, remind me that You are with me when I experience doubt and disappointment. As I look at my wounds, help me see the victorious marks in Jesus' hands and side. Renew my enthusiasm for ministry. In Jesus' name. Amen.

~ 9 ~

Bury the Body and Go Tell Jesus

John's disciples came and took his body and buried it.
Then they went and told Jesus. Matthew 14:12

When the reality of the crisis finally hit, we fell silent. The contractor we had hired to build a new sanctuary had run off with $200,000 of the church's money. A letter went out the next day inviting members to a special meeting where the congregation's leadership would share the "gory" details of the sad tale.

Our average attendance at congregational meetings was about 150. Almost 400 people came to hear the bad news and share their anger and criticism. Person after person rose to speak of their incredulity that something like this could happen. It was a sad day.

After a few hours of wailing and gnashing of teeth, a lady asked, "Pastor, what do you think we should do?" Sometimes the Holy Spirit makes us wiser than we really are. The Spirit did that for me. For some reason, I opened my Bible to Matthew 14, the story of the death of John the Baptist. I said, "I think we should follow the example of the disciples after the death of John the Baptist. They buried John's body, then they told Jesus."

The death of John the Baptist was a crisis for John's followers. Evil appeared to reign. They could have asked Jesus why He didn't see this tragedy coming and do something about it. They could have wondered if their confidence in Jesus' leadership was misplaced. They could have done all these things; they did none of them. Instead, they buried John and told Jesus about it.

24

John's disciples established a model for those who deal with disappointment and disaster in the church. Church workers and those we serve could repudiate, threaten, humiliate, and otherwise try to hurt those who fail us or make mistakes. But such behavior is beneath the children of God. In Christ, we don't have time to dwell on harm done. Instead, we remind ourselves that all have sinned and fallen short of God's glory. But Jesus bridged the gap created by sin.

The shortcomings of others lose their sting in light of God's Word. We can do what John's disciples did: We can bury the body, whether it's a fiscal year in the red, an inability to reach attendance goals, or a conflict that causes members to leave. Whatever the situation, we who trust in our Lord and His resurrection bury the body and tell Jesus.

The growth of God's kingdom did not end with the death of John the Baptist. To the contrary, the kingdom grew. The growth of our churches and ministries will not end because of our troubles. On the contrary, the Lord of Life, to whom we take our anger, will pick us up, calm us down, and make us more effective than before.

So as a congregation, we buried the tragedy. We determined together that we would put this behind us, then we told Jesus. Jesus strengthened us, and we re-entered the construction process, filled with enthusiasm. Next time you're in town, come see our new sanctuary.

The Prayer: Jesus, You make all things new. Help me and those I serve do as John's disciples did when they faced injustice—bury the body and tell You. Strengthen me to follow this model daily so my ministry might continue uninterrupted for Your glory. In Your name. Amen.

~ 10 ~

How to Speak So People Will Listen

A word aptly spoken is like apples of gold in settings of silver. *Proverbs 25:11*

With four children in our family, listening is essential. Many are the moments when all four children and my wife vie simultaneously for my ear. Inevitably, one person isn't heard. Often that person is the one whose story I selfishly regard as least important. In our household, that person simply stands up and says, "Excuse me, but I believe it is my turn to be heard." That is everyone's cue to refocus attention.

The congregations we serve often are like large families that constantly engage in conversation. Church leaders talk to one another about church business. Members speak to one another and sometimes to the pastor about church business. Choir members talk, the youth talk, even those who do not attend services talk about what is or isn't going on in church. These conversations are full of hopes, dreams, opinions, attitudes, complaints, and disappointments.

Yet there always are some people in the congregation who get no one's attention. Often the people who are not heard are teachers, deaconesses, or DCEs. These people are left to struggle with how they are to be heard by those who called them to serve. Some try to organize support groups for their point of view and let advocates speak for them. Others stand up as voices crying alone in the wilderness. Historically, neither is an effective approach for getting heard. Instead, these approaches can cause a schism.

Jesus encourages us to stand up within our congregations and say, "Excuse me, but I believe it is my turn to be heard." Surprising as it may sound, Jesus' words from the cross give us words to be heard in our churches and a posture to assume as we speak them.

Writing about our Lord, St. Paul said: "Your attitude should be the same as that of Christ Jesus: Who, being in very nature God, did not consider equality with God something to be grasped, but made Himself nothing, taking the very nature of a servant, being made in human likeness. And being found in appearance as a man, He humbled Himself and became obedient to death—even death on a cross!" (Philippians 2:5–8). Paul goes on to say that it was Jesus' humility that exalted Him. As church workers, we are not above our Master. Humility is also our posture. We may not be heard on the street or in the political arena, but humble people will be heard in the church.

God's Word and Jesus' attitude should be part of our vocabularies and our lifestyles if we want to be heard. Who wouldn't listen to someone who forgives in Jesus' name? Who wouldn't listen to someone who commits life and spirit into God's hands? Who wouldn't listen to someone who fulfills responsibilities and obligations, even toward family? Who wouldn't listen to someone who thirsts for the opportunity to serve? Church members search for people like this so they can listen to them.

The Jesus who lives inside us is working to make us people who imitate His attitude and speech. When we speak and live like Jesus, our words aren't just heard, they are sought. May God grant this to us in our ministries.

The Prayer: Lord Jesus, I long to be heard by the people I serve. Cause me to listen more than I speak, to forgive more than I hold grudges, to fulfill my responsibilities and obligations, and to thirst for righteousness so the people I serve may see You in me. In Jesus' holy name. Amen.

~ 11 ~

Retreat!

Yet the news about [Jesus] spread all the more, so that crowds of people came to hear Him and to be healed of their sicknesses. But Jesus often withdrew to lonely places and prayed. *Luke 5:15–16*

Imagine that for the last 20 years you have cared for a paralyzed uncle. You have dressed, fed, and carried him wherever he has wished to go. Your life has been hard.

Then you hear news that Jesus of Nazareth has been healing people. You hear that Jesus will be in your neighborhood. You dress your uncle and take him to see Jesus. When you arrive, you're at the end of a long line of ailing people. As the sun goes down, you have moved close enough to see Jesus for the first time. You and your uncle begin to rejoice. In just a few moments, both of you will be free from this encumbrance. You see Jesus place His hands on a blind woman, and she receives her sight. She moves and leaves you and your uncle in front of Jesus.

Jesus sighs deeply. You see the fatigue in His eyes. He seems relieved that you're the last in line. Hands trembling with weariness, Jesus touches your uncle. The paralysis quivers out of his body. Before you can praise Him, Jesus turns and addresses His disciples. He says something about being exhausted and needing a quiet place to pray.

You understand. If Jesus remains, He can expect another surge of "patients." He must leave now. He needs strength for the difficult days ahead. His Father appointed a future time and place where Jesus would need all His strength to take away the world's sin.

Scripture is clear. Jesus sometimes retreated from the crowds. He rested and prayed. Disappointed people desperately would search for Him, seeking relief from various infirmities. But Jesus knew when He needed rest. It's an important lesson for church workers to learn.

Jesus does not expect us to work all the time. We want to work hard for the people we serve, but we also have the right and responsibility to retreat—to renew our energy through rest, privacy, family time, Bible study, and prayer. In fact, learning and responding to our limits gives glory and honor to God. We care for ourselves in a way that promotes better service in God's kingdom.

Some time ago, I attended the funeral of a pastor. I looked at his wife and three young children during the service. They heard parishioners share their sorrow and speak glowingly of how this man always put the church first, even before his own health. I thought, "His priorities may have contributed to his death. This church will have another pastor within six months, but this family will never have him back again. I wish he had rested more."

God frees us to relax from our ministries. We can balance our schedules. Sometimes we need to say no to requests. Our no allows the Spirit to use other people to accomplish His plans. Our no gives us time to withdraw, study His Word, and pray. It gives us time to reflect on Christ's death and resurrection to save us and those we serve. May God grant us the faith and strength to rest and to say an appropriate no.

The Prayer: O Lord, thank You for the stories of Your ministry. They let me see my need to rest and pray. Take away any guilt that the devil sows during my moments of rest. Let me see that in saying no, I actually open the door for others to serve and honor You. In Your name. Amen.

~ 12 ~

Dos and Deeds of Reconciliation

"If your brother sins against you, go and show him his fault, just between the two of you. If he listens to you, you have won your brother over." *Matthew 18:15*

In my first parish, the senior pastor welcomed me with open arms. However, it didn't take long before he started doing some things that irritated me. For example, if I walked into a meeting a minute or two late, he would poke fun at me. At other gatherings, he teased me in front of the people I was called to serve. He invited laughter about the length of my sermons or prayers—or in those days, the length of my hair.

Matthew 18:15–16 made my next step in the unfortunate situation painfully clear. I needed to tell him what was bothering me. I nervously set up the appointment, all the while wondering if this conversation would make things worse and perhaps even end my ministry in that place.

When I presented myself for our meeting, before I knew it, the words were out: "I appreciate the opportunity I have for ministry here with you, but I really don't appreciate being the brunt of your jokes." We talked, and God acted. We left that meeting tremendous friends with a strengthened commitment to our joint ministry and a renewed respect for each other.

Are you in conflict with anyone in your church? Has it gone on for a long time and you haven't tried to resolve it? Have you chosen to hope the problem will die of old age? (Problems never die of old age, only people do that.) Do some teachers always miss their turn at supervising the playground? Do coworkers conveniently forget to do what you've asked? Do some faculty members hold "meetings" after the faculty meeting? Would you like these things to end?

Read Matthew 18. Recall that Jesus is the Lord of the Church, pray for a humble Spirit and a double measure of love, and speak to them. Ask the Lord to fill your tongue with the same kindness and love that He practiced and preached—even from the cross. Then stand back and watch Jesus work His miracle of reconciliation. (By the way, ask Jesus to open your heart if you've been a problem to others. Be open to receive feedback as well as to give it.) Jesus calls together persons in conflict to give them healing words and loving ears to hear what is said with thanksgiving. Jesus lifts reconciled people up as models of Christian life and witnesses to His presence and power.

May the Spirit of God move so powerfully among church workers that agonizing divisions are not found among us.

The Prayer: Gracious Jesus, Scripture declares how good it is when brothers and sisters live together in peace and unity. Remind me again that Your power is sufficient to break down my fear of speaking to those who have offended me. Fill me with grace when others confront me. Give me confidence in Your presence and the words to speak that will restore unity and bring You the glory. In Jesus' name. Amen.

~ 13 ~

O Lord, Please Close Our Lips ...
Sometimes

"You shall not give false testimony against your neighbor." *Exodus 20:16*

Nobody obeys the Ten Commandments, but some have been ignored into obscurity. Take, for example, the Fifth Commandment. Daily headlines confirm that people often disobey this commandment. However, to ignore the Fifth Commandment would lead to anarchy.

How different this is from the way society deals with the Sixth Commandment. We observe rampant rates of divorce, sexual promiscuity, and couples living together outside of marriage. Yet few people raise an eyebrow at these activities. In general, our society embraces this sin and has legitimized it.

Some of us are outraged at those who break the Sixth Commandment, but who of us shows the same outrage when the Eighth Commandment is broken? I submit that more than one issue of those sensational tabloids have worked their way into Christian living rooms. Church parking lots are convenient places to leave your car, but they also serve as sites for gossip and criticism of those who aren't present to defend themselves.

The behavior of some Christians suggests that we have legitimized disobedience of the Eighth Commandment. In fact, some people believe they have an obligation to speak evil against those who have "rubbed them the wrong way." They believe such action "warns" people about the faults of others. Gossip, which is forbidden in the Eighth Commandment, threatens the health and well-being of God's Church. But gossip isn't something individuals can do by themselves!

Jesus has made us new people through His death and resurrection. Accusations from our enemies, especially the devil, will not stick to us throughout eternity. In thanksgiving to God for our "redeemed" reputations, church workers get to serve as a type of "gossip squad." God's grace sends us into the world with a good word to share about our neighbors, a word just as good as the word Jesus speaks about us. As church workers, God has placed us into communities of faith where we can build up people.

Affirming the pastoral staff makes pastors feel appreciated and willing to work that much harder for the people they love. Saying positive things about the church staff enables them to answer phones and prepare service folders with a positive and helpful spirit. Saying positive things about the school faculty strengthens them to work harder for children and families.

Jesus called us to bring positive attitudes about coworkers to our churches. At the same time, He called us to discourage those who gossip. Jesus, whose death and resurrection redeemed our good names, would have us honor Him by refusing to listen to malicious or demeaning statements about any brother or sister, pastor or teacher, parent or child.

An article I wrote suggested that Jesus has put such tremendous news on our lips that we don't have to waste time talking about others. Shortly after the newsletter was mailed, an indignant woman said, "Pastor, your article was ludicrous. If we can't talk about each other, all we've got left to talk about is God, and what kind of a life is that?"

It's a wonderful life! It's our life as church workers. Talking about God and how He has blessed us through the people we serve causes others to speak well also. This makes Psalm 133:1 a reality: "How good and pleasant it is when brothers live together in unity!"

The Prayer: God in heaven, Jesus taught us to pray, "Thy will be done on earth as it is in heaven." Let this happen in every area of my life, but especially in my speech. Let Your Spirit encourage me to be an example of love and grace in the way I talk about my coworkers, the people I serve, and even my detractors. In Jesus' name. Amen.

~ 14 ~

Honor Your Father and Mother ... and Teacher

"Honor your father and your mother, so that you may
live long in the land the LORD your God is giving you."
Exodus 20:12

When the pastor is called into a meeting between parents, principal, and teacher, unpleasantries are a certainty. After one such meeting, I said to the principal, "We need to include one more question on our application for enrollment."

"What would that question be," she asked?

"Simple. Is your child perfect, yes or no?" We laughed, but the implication of this "joke" is serious.

Some parents hold their children in much higher moral and ethical esteem than appropriate. "For all have sinned and fall short of the glory of God" (Romans 3:23) sometimes doesn't affect parents' evaluation of their children. At the same time, parents often hold teachers and preachers in lower regard than the Scriptures do: "Remember your leaders, who spoke the word of God to you. Consider the outcome of their way of life and imitate their faith" (Hebrews 13:7). In situations such as these, conflicts are inevitable.

The center or focus of the conflict is always critical. Until we determine the center, the conflict can't be resolved in a God-pleasing manner. A student's behavior does not often lie at the center of the conflict; instead, the conflict revolves around parental guilt and shame. Parents sometimes "justify" themselves and their failures by criticizing those who discipline their children.

It's easy to criticize defensive parents and label them as crazy or irrational. Such labeling may make us feel better, but it does absolutely no good for the child or the parents. As Christian preachers and teachers, we do what we can to help families keep the Fourth Commandment. Families will be happier and healthier when they honor those whom God has placed in positions of authority, including teachers and pastors.

When confronted by the parents of "perfect" children, we pray that Jesus will remind us that He prayed, "Father, forgive them." We bear the unbearable; we speak no unkind word. We remember these people in our prayers. We ask God to keep us from pouting, gossiping, or abandoning them. Instead, we ask Jesus to enable us to speak well of them and hold them in love and esteem. We ask Him to change their hearts as He has changed us by the Gospel. By the power of the Holy Spirit and the love of Jesus, they do change. Through our love and devotion, they sense that we know their secret: Their children really aren't perfect and neither are they. Perhaps for the first time in their lives, these people may experience the joy of unconditional love.

Some schools insist that students and parents meet the highest standards before they are admitted. As servants of Christ, we open our doors to sinners who think they are perfect with the knowledge that Christ's love working through the Word will make them perfect through faith.

The Prayer: Lord, send me "perfect" kids, and strengthen me to minister to them and their parents. Then they can drop their defenses, confess their sins, and rejoice in the true perfection Jesus has secured for them. In His name. Amen.

~ 15 ~

Remembering the Sabbath

Then [Jesus] said to them, "The Sabbath was made for man, not man for the Sabbath. So the Son of Man is Lord even of the Sabbath." *Mark 2:27–28*

"Pastor, God was good to us this Christmas season. We sold every tree we could get our hands on, but I've kept two real pretty trees for the church. I'd like to donate them. Would that be all right?"

How could I refuse this generous offer? I knew this was breaking new ground. Our church had never had two Christmas trees in the chancel before. This year would be different. This man's generosity and God's bounty would make it so!

The trees were delivered and decorated. The chancel was absolutely gorgeous. Knowing this, you can understand my surprise when I heard that members were circulating a petition to prevent two trees in the chancel ever again. The petition read: "There is one baby Jesus, one manger, one star of Bethlehem, one mother, one Father; therefore, there should be one Christmas tree in our church's chancel." I was tempted to ask about the multiple shepherds and Wise Men, but I decided on discretion instead.

To place this problem in context of the above Scripture reading, the two trees violated a Sabbath law. The benefactor who gave us the trees was heartbroken. He had no idea that his generosity would lead to conflict. I was angry and disappointed. I wanted to approach the signers of this petition and ask, "Was the Sabbath created for man or was man created for the Sabbath?" I didn't do that.

I took time to think and pray about what this passage means. It means that people take precedence over rituals—or changes in rituals. It means that people, not laws, are to be the object of our love—even those people who don't want two Christmas trees in the chancel.

The special congregational meeting that dealt with this "crisis" gave me an opportunity to make this point. Since Jesus gave no clear command on the subject of Christmas trees in the chancel, the church was free to do what it wanted. The trees were not the issue. The issue was the wonderful people of God who wanted to honor Jesus through a beautiful chancel. We took pains to ensure that no one's feelings were hurt in the discussion. I sat in awe as people grew together in love and concern for one another. The hostility and division as people entered the meeting gave way to sincere love and concern for the well-being of brothers and sisters in Christ.

The meeting ended when the man who donated the trees apologized. No sooner had he sat down than the lady who had circulated the petition said, "No person in this church should ever have to apologize for giving a gift to Jesus." She apologized. Before we knew it, the congregation forgot this divisive issue. However, we remembered how Jesus taught us that people are more important than tradition or innovation.

Each of us serves a church where traditions sometimes assume divine status. This devotion to tradition can get in the way of ministry. Jesus refocuses us on what is always of major concern: the proclamation of His Word and the care of His people. May God always keep His professional church workers focused on His Word and His people—willing to endure change for their sake. Then we will see what is more important than trees, traditions, egos, or Sabbath laws. May we all clearly take the side of Jesus on any issue regarding traditions. And may our primary focus remain on salvation through Jesus Christ.

The Prayer: Dear God, Your Word makes Your priorities clear. You love Your people. You gave Your Law to bless people. Don't allow my commitment to traditions hurt people or keep them from seeing Your salvation. Make my church a place where Your love is always obvious. In Jesus' name. Amen.

~16~

Team Sports

We who are strong ought to bear with the failings of the weak and not to please ourselves. Each of us should please his neighbor for his good, to build him up.
Romans 15:1–2

Team sports aren't for everyone. Team sports emphasize the greatness of the team as a whole, not just one team member. Team sports spread the responsibility around when a game is lost. Team sports help develop lifelong relationships of trust and confidence.

Church work is a team sport. Jesus made that clear from the beginning. He didn't undertake His ministry alone. He gathered to Himself 12 disciples (later 70 disciples) who prepared the way for Him.

Team ministries are wonderful, but sometimes they become unbearably frustrating. The frustration occurs when people don't do their jobs. In other words, they fail. Sometimes people are repentant. Other times, they seem blissfully unaware of their failures. In fact, sometimes the failure is habitual. They *never* get to faculty meetings on time; they *never* take recess duty; they *never* attend special church services. These failures can lead to horrible divisions within a church or school staff … unless those staff members realize two eternal truths.

The first truth is "There but for the grace of God go I." We may not duplicate the failures of our colleagues, but we all fail occasionally. The second truth is a reminder not to judge others. The time we spend trying to document and announce the sins of coworkers could be better spent improving our own ministry.

I enjoy watching the young people of our junior high school during recess and physical education. They concentrate on demonstrating their emerging strength, which is determined by pounds lifted, inches and feet jumped, or distances covered in short periods of time. In the kingdom of God, our Scripture lesson teaches that strength is demonstrated in the way we deal with the failures of others.

We can't be strong on our own, but the Spirit that lives within us is the Holy Spirit, who knows all there is to know about the failures of His "team." Even on the night Jesus was betrayed, when He turned to His closest friends and followers, they failed Him. Instead of fussing about their failures, Jesus continued with the mission that God had entrusted to Him. He secured the salvation of the world. After accomplishing His task, Jesus dealt in love with those who had failed Him. His love kept them from being destroyed by their failures. In fact, His love and forgiveness helped them grow through their mistakes.

The same thing happens in the church today when we forgive those who have failed us. When we don't bring shame to those who disappoint us but work to support them in ministry, the church and our coworkers grow. Each of us has daily opportunities to show the strength of God's people by dealing with the failures of coworkers. Guess what? Our posture of love amazes people and shows them Jesus. Thanks be to God!

The Prayer: O Lord, make me strong in faith, love, and patience. I ask for this strength as I daily deal with people who fail me. Help me to leave my self-righteous position of supremacy by remembering that I have failed and fallen short of Your glory. Let me show the strength You give as I love, support, pray for, and speak well of all those with whom I work. In Jesus' name. Amen.

Righteous Anger

"In your anger do not sin": Do not let the sun go down while you are still angry. *Ephesians 4:26*

Despite popular opinion, people of God get angry occasionally. Our non-Christian detractors may enjoy this. In their minds, Christians should be "perfect" people. Anger doesn't fit their understanding of perfection. Being identified as Christians, at least by the virtue of our work, we might be intimidated by those who don't think anger is consistent with faithfulness to Jesus.

Such intimidation should stop for the sake of Jesus and His church. Anger is not a sinful thing in and of itself. Our Lord Jesus lived without sin, but when His mother impatiently insisted that He help the bride and groom at Cana, He took exception to her pleas. When the disciples couldn't understand His teaching, He said, "How much longer will I have to put up with you?" And when merchants turned the temple into a marketplace, Jesus angrily drove the money-changers from His Father's house.

Anger is permissible for Christians. How do Christians committed to the nurture of children not get angry when they hear about child abuse? How do Christian social workers avoid anger when gangs threaten the children they serve? How can Christian church workers not get angry at people who are determined to create dissension in the church?

Christians need to get angry occasionally. To avoid anger is to lose one's perspective of right and wrong. Anger is not a sin. The sin comes when it's time to do something about that anger. Paul, the author of Ephesians, says it best:

" 'In your anger, do not sin': Do not let the sun go down while you are still angry." Most of us can endure unjust and abusive behavior for a time. But eventually it builds to an explosion. The Bible instructs us to deal with our anger as it builds.

We serve Jesus when we stay after school and talk to the principal who has unfairly accused us of wrongdoing. We serve Jesus when we tell the pastor with whom we plan the worship service that he treats us unfairly and unprofessionally. We serve Jesus when we tell parents that we don't appreciate what they told their children to do. In each case, we are angry, but we are not sinning. The sun is not going down on our anger. We are dealing with our neighbors with respect, trusting their maturity. Jesus expressed His feelings, even the angry ones. His anger was always fair and just. He will help our lives and ministries run smoother as we follow His example.

Generally speaking, many people fear that if they confront a problem head on, they will destroy relationships and upset people. Jesus will give His people wisdom and grace and help them reconcile their relationships just as He reconciled us with God. May God give us grace to see such things happen in our lives and ministries.

The Prayer: Dear Jesus, take away my fear of anger. Help me remember that You, too, were angry and used Your anger constructively for the kingdom's sake. Help me learn how to share anger and receive it in ways that build up Your kingdom and Your people. In Your name. Amen.

~ 18 ~

Tired and Weary

Do you not know? Have you not heard? The LORD is the everlasting God, the Creator of the ends of the earth. He will not grow tired or weary, and His understanding no one can fathom. He gives strength to the weary and increases the power of the weak. *Isaiah 40:28–29*

The people of God say many things to their church workers. Some examples include "Nice sermon." "That service was too long." "Thanks for all you did for my child this year." "Do you need help in the classroom?" Some of what we hear is positive. Some of what people say expresses their wonder at what the Lord enables us to accomplish. "I don't see how you do everything that you do!" is something I hear said to church workers.

Most church workers just shrug their shoulders and thank those who say such nice words. Church workers say little, and what they seem never to share is how tired they get doing what congregations call them to do. It is not unusual for church workers to teach all day, correct papers for an hour or two, then direct the choir and finish up the night with more papers or lesson plans.

We get tired, but we keep going. Our tendency to keep going can be good or bad. It's bad if we keep going because we believe we are the only person who can accomplish what needs to be done. Getting tired because we think that the success or failure of our ministry depends only on our strength, commitment, gifts, and will is unhealthy and leads to burnout.

Getting tired because we enjoy what we're doing and receive satisfaction from the service we are privileged to perform is good. Those who know they aren't solely responsible for their ministry's success find satisfaction in ministry. God is the One who is responsible. Those who follow God's lead, doing what He initiates and trusting Him for success, find their strength renewed regularly by God.

This is the good news that Isaiah brought to Israel and to us: "He gives strength to the weary and increases the power of the weak." This strength comes from knowing that God blesses and completes everything we do in Jesus' name. These are great words for church workers. God uses them to establish boundaries regarding what we should do in our ministries and what He will do. For our part, we turn it over to God and do our best.

Isaiah confesses that he is in trouble with God because of his unclean lips. Isaiah confesses that he doesn't measure up to what God wants him to be. Scripture also records that Isaiah accomplished tremendous things for God's people, especially providing faithful prophecies about the Savior. Paul declares in Romans 7 that the good he would do, he does not do, and the evil he would not do, he does. He's not satisfied with his progress. But God steps in and makes him the most powerful missionary the church has ever known. Once they had tasted the grace of God, both Paul and Isaiah relaxed in His power and trusted Him to reach His goals through them.

It is the very same thing for each of us. We receive the Christ-secured opportunity to rest in God. We trust His power to make us a blessing. We can even dream and wonder how God will make good all our work. Thanks to Jesus, we can be so secure in God's ability to overcome our shortcomings that we feel strong and confident as we undertake the next project for His kingdom. May God enable us to remember that He is the one who restores strength to the weary as we depend completely on Him.

The Prayer: Lord, I get tired—sometimes for the right reasons, and sometimes for the wrong reasons. Help me to avoid the fatigue that comes when I believe that everything depends on me. Help me to realize the blessed weariness that comes to those who freely and confidently work to serve You, trusting that You will accomplish far more than I can imagine. In Your name. Amen.

~ 19 ~

Give Them What You Have

Another of His disciples, Andrew, Simon Peter's broth-er, spoke up, "Here is a boy with five small barley loaves and two small fish, but how far will they go among so many?" John 6:8–9

I think about this story every time our congregation prepares its annual budget. We ask those responsible for different ministries to project the funds they need to carry out their service to God. The numbers are always enthusiastic. Then we compare the dollars hoped for to the promises given by contributors. Sometimes we've been as far as $200,000 apart. That's when I have to announce that we won't have enough money to do all that we want. Then I speak to God as Andrew did: "Lord, we have 'x' dollars, but what are they among so many?"

Jesus' response to me is the same one He gave to Philip: "Give what you have and that will be enough." It's never what our staff wants to hear, but it's always the truth. Give what you have, and Jesus will make sure it's enough. This is our Lord's word when we feel we don't have the resources to do what we want.

It may be a shortage of time, money, passion, or com-passion, but Jesus always behaves as He did when He fed more than 5,000 people. He tells us to bring our loaves and fish, time and money, hope and patience, love and self-con-trol. Then He blesses it and makes it enough. His blessing is the difference between famine and plenty.

God has never kept His power to Himself. He used it to create this world. He guided people through the leadership of nondescript shepherds such as Moses and David. He brought His Word to bear against the kings of Israel through the likes of the fig-splitter Amos. In a simple manger, He presented the Savior to the world. In each of these cases, God took what looked too small for the task, blessed it, and caused it to accomplish His will.

Some people, including church workers, are embarrassed about what they bring to the Lord. They believe their time, expertise, paycheck, and even their faith are not sufficient. Nothing could be further from the truth. Jesus, who offered His life on the cross, touched death and made it the gateway to eternal life. Now He sits at the right hand of God the Father and touches each one of our offerings. His touch makes each offering more than enough.

The four evangelists tell about the life of our Lord according to the needs of the people for whom they originally wrote. It's not a coincidence that they don't tell us about all the same events. But they all tell the feeding of the 5,000. Perhaps God knew we would need a reminder, through this story, that we can give Him what we have and know that He will make it enough.

The Prayer: Dear Lord, today I want to be like the young boy who gave You his lunch. You blessed his gift and used it to show Your power to the world. Take my gifts, bless them, and use them to show Your power to the world. In Your name. Amen.

~20~
The Rest of the Story

*Now the serpent was more crafty than any of the wild animals the L*ORD *God had made. He said to the woman, "Did God really say, 'You must not eat from any tree in the garden'?" Genesis 3:1*

With this question, the devil encouraged Eve to doubt. She suspected that her life was not as wonderful as it could be and that God was the reason for her lack of complete happiness. She learned of the devil's deception the moment she ate the fruit. Together with her husband, who also ate the fruit, she faced the consequences of her behavior. God articulated those consequences with these words: "I will greatly increase your pains in childbearing; with pain you will give birth to children. Your desire will be for your husband, and he will rule over you" (Genesis 3:16).

Certainly the Bible conveys everything we need to know about God, but sometimes I wonder if the Bible doesn't omit some of the story. I particularly wonder about this story. After God told Eve that her life would be changed forever, I wonder if the devil didn't visit her again and ask the same question: "Did God really say that your life will be changed forever?" I ask this question because of the behavior of Adam and Eve's children—people like you and me.

The Fall affected all creation. The Fall, when properly understood, explains the reasons for tragedies. Wars, famines, earthquakes, and death result from the disjointedness that exists between people and this world because of sin. Smaller crises in life such as financial difficulties, marital strife, and children who misbehave happen to everyone as a result of sin. And just as in Eve's case, you have to wonder if the devil doesn't ask: "Did God really say you were going to have trouble in your life?" He might lead you to ask: "Why is God doing this to me?" or "What did I do to deserve this?"

The devil tempts church workers as well. He encourages us to look at others and ask, "Why am I not paid what I'm worth?" Because of sin. "Why am I in conflict with my pastor, my staff, the teachers, my DCE, my deaconess, my principal?" Because of sin. We need not be surprised when people anger or disappoint us. God said that we would have trouble.

But that wasn't God's last word to us. In Romans 8:28, God tells us the rest of the story. "And we know that in all things God works for the good of those who love Him, who have been called according to His purpose." And verses 31, 32, 35, and 37–38:

> What, then, shall we say in response to this? If God is for us, who can be against us? He who did not spare His own Son, but gave Him up for us all—how will He not also, along with Him, graciously give us all things? ... Who shall separate us from the love of Christ? Shall trouble or hardship or persecution or famine or nakedness or danger or sword? ... No, in all these things we are more than conquerors through Him who loved us. For I am convinced that neither death nor life, neither angels nor demons, neither the present nor the future, nor any powers, neither height nor depth, nor anything else in all creation, will be able to separate us from the love of God that is in Christ Jesus our Lord.

One great thing about working for Jesus is that when the devil tempts us with seductive questions, we know the rest of the story. We know that conflict is inevitable and victory over that conflict is assured in Christ.

One reason the church is in a crisis regarding the recruitment of professional workers is that young people see pastors and teachers who aren't happy. They aren't happy because their lives and ministries didn't turn out the way they wanted. For many reasons, these potential role models fail to rejoice that Jesus makes us more than conquerors.

Jesus calls us to live the full story: We are hurt, but we will be healed. We may be depressed, but hope is ours. God said we'd have trouble as a result of the Fall, but even more loudly He said we are more than conquerors through Jesus who loves us. Most days we do a wonderful job of telling the rest of the story. Today we pray that God will enable us to live the story through lives of hope, love, joy—lives that reflect the Good News that Jesus is our Savior.

The Prayer: Dear Lord, I sometimes feel I don't deserve the trouble I experience. Help me to accept trouble without becoming angry, hopeless, or selfish. Instead, let me remember the rest of the story—that I am more than a conqueror through You. Use me to make that victory obvious to those I serve. In Jesus' name. Amen.

~ 21 ~

Faithful into the Future

Be faithful, even to the point of death, and I will give you the crown of life. *Revelation 2:10*

Someone defined *tradition* as the living faith of the dead and the dead faith of the living. These are strong words. They might hurt our feelings and make us defensive of the way we've always done things. They are also wise words that will keep us from allowing our faith and our ministries to become obsolete.

The book of Proverbs encourages God's people regarding words such as these when it says: "Do not rebuke a mocker or he will hate you; rebuke a wise man and he will love you. Instruct a wise man and he will be wiser still; teach a righteous man and he will add to his learning" (Proverbs 9:8–9). People who trust Jesus can give up traditions to be faithful to the Gospel. Blessed are the people who have the courage to be faithful and change the way they do things—if that change brings the Gospel to the world.

As a youngster, I remember that the most difficult time of the worship service was Communion distribution. In my childhood, children were expected to sit reverently while their parents went to the altar. When my parents dropped to their knees at the altar, their backs were turned. It was a perfect time for my brother and me to fight. My little brother quickly learned not to tell because it was his word against mine. The sad thing is that we missed the importance of what was happening at the altar.

Today, my children approach the altar to receive a blessing during distribution. Someone had the courage to suggest this change. I'm sure they were criticized, but the change has been a blessing to thousands of young people, who now see they are welcome at God's altar.

Jesus calls church workers to courageously develop innovations that will bring the Gospel to more people. Those who minister at the dawn of a new century want to use the minds God has given them to find new ways to include people in the fellowship of faith. The possibilities are endless:

- A confirmation program that wraps the dimensions of love and service around a faithful study of Bible and confession enables today's children to embrace faith enthusiastically.

- A Web site designed to occupy latch-key kids in the community tells families that Jesus cares about them.

- A change in the time-honored worship schedule, Bible study method, or fellowship ministries to better serve today's frantic families demonstrates a faithfulness that reflects God's Word.

The Holy Spirit will lead and guide each of us who are privileged to serve our Lord professionally as we eagerly look to the needs of those we serve and develop appropriate, effective ways to declare that Jesus is Savior and Lord. May the Lord of the Church keep us faithful not just to our traditions, but to Him. In faith, we look forward to our crown of life.

The Prayer: Lord Jesus, You know how hard change is for me. Give me courage, wisdom, and the power of Your Spirit to tailor my service to the needs of Your people. In so doing, I know that I will show them Your love. Grant this, Lord, for Your sake. Amen.

Gracious Words Part 1

Do not let any unwholesome talk come out of your mouths, but only what is helpful for building others up according to their needs, that it may benefit those who listen. *Ephesians 4:29*

Growing up, my parents taught me there were two "magic" words that opened life's doors. One of them was *please*. I learned this lesson well. I said please before I did anything. That was appropriate when one desires seconds, freedom to play with friends, or approval to change the TV station. It's not appropriate, however, when your dentist asks if you're ready for your tooth to be drilled. But I said it anyway. For a long time, I thought my folks overdid it a little with that lesson. I don't think so anymore.

I changed my mind because *please* has become a seldom-used word. Has the federal government asked permission to raise our taxes? Has a telemarketer asked permission to call you during dinner? Has someone's child asked to raid your refrigerator? Presumptuous acts such as these happen far too frequently.

I've also learned that *please* isn't a magic word. It's a heart word—a gracious word, a word of respect. People who ask us for permission before they do something demonstrate that they care about us. Polite speech indicates that we're not here to force our will on people; instead, we are here to help.

The apostle Paul, in addressing the church at Ephesus, encourages Christians to avoid unwholesome talk and to say only what is helpful for building up others. Unwholesome talk can be considered vile speech, but it goes further than that. Any speech that turns people into objects tears them down.

As church workers, our goal is to build up people; therefore, we become people who say *please* when we have the opportunity. A saying sometimes used among pastors says, "It's always better to say 'I'm sorry' than to say 'please.' " I can understand the desire to get things done in a timely fashion, but our text suggests that such thinking does more to tear down people than it does to build them up. School teachers whose job it is to build up students use the word *please* repeatedly—even when they ask the class to be quiet.

I'll never forget calling the mother of one of my playmates to ask if I could *please* speak with him. She responded, "It is so refreshing to hear a young person be so polite." Jesus enables us to be a breath of fresh air to our world. Using *please* may seem inconsequential, but in a world where people often are taken for granted, it makes an impression. The impression we give is not only of ourselves, but more important, of Jesus—the King of kings who gave His life for us. Today, for Jesus' sake, make your speech wholesome ... please?

The Prayer: Gracious God, You love every person. Because they are Yours, they deserve my respect. Let my speech always be instructed by the Spirit so all my words are gracious. In Jesus' name and for His sake. Amen.

~23~

Gracious Words Part 2

I thank my God every time I remember you.
Philippians 1:3

A psychologist told me that the best indicator of a person's maturity is his or her ability to postpone gratification. People who are well-adjusted can wait for things they would like to have now. People who are poorly adjusted need to have what they want immediately.

I believe there is a way to observe the spiritual maturity of a person too. It has nothing to do with postponing gratification, however. It has everything to do with showing gratification by saying, "Thank you."

Those who acknowledge the gifts and assistance they receive from others demonstrate the same heart and spirit as the apostle Paul. Paul wanted to give the church at Philippi instructions regarding the Christian life, but he began by thanking them for their grace and generosity in sending him a gift while he was in prison. This gesture of love filled Paul's heart and mind, and he wanted to thank them before he said anything else.

As Christians who are growing in grace, we realize we owe God an incredible debt of thanks. Not only has He saved us from sin, death, and the power of the devil, He daily provides us with all that we need to support our life. We properly can offer our prayers from a position of thankfulness. When we are thankful, then we are humble. When we are humble, people can see the love of Christ in us.

Mature Christians also see the effort other Christians offer in service to God. When we see this service, we can take time to thank them. I once asked a dear Christian woman who served hard in her church why she gave so much of herself. Her answer was eye opening. She said, "I work hard because Jesus loves me. Besides that, people here appreciate me." She went on to share the great number of thank-you notes and cards she had received from the pastors and leaders of that church. Better than that, she gave credit to God for the good she did.

Spiritually mature people do things that spiritually immature people do not do. One of those things is expressing thankfulness. If you haven't done it already, buy thank-you cards and write one each day. Your card will encourage the people to whom you write as much as Paul's words encouraged the church at Philippi. And perhaps something even more important will happen.

When your goal is to write one thank-you note each day, you begin to develop an eye that concentrates on the wonderful things God does through people. Seeing and appreciating the sacrifices of others inspires us. Our joy becomes complete so we can join Paul when he says to the Philippians: "Rejoice in the Lord always. I will say it again: Rejoice!" (Philippians 4:4). Concentrating on the positive things that God does through people fills us with joy.

When you are floundering in ministry, wondering what you're accomplishing, remember Paul's words. Write someone a thank-you note or thank someone face to face. Tell people that you thank God for them.

The Prayer: Dear Father in heaven, help me grow in Your grace to become a thankful person. Open my eyes so I can see the wonderful work that You do through others in the kingdom. Help me learn to use the words "thank you" at every appropriate moment. Use those words from my lips and heart to build up Your people. Thank You, Jesus. Amen.

~24~

Another Gracious Word

Forgive us our debts, as we also have forgiven our debtors. Matthew 6:12

I love college football, especially the Rose Bowl. I love the game and the pageantry, but I am not crazy about the crowd. The crowds begin the minute you enter the tunnel to get to your seats. Most years, the crowd pushes. People think the more they push, the faster they will get to their seats. What these "pushers" don't understand is that they create a sense of uneasiness that borders on hysteria.

Last year I was sure that those who pushed and shoved were going to force a stampede. Just as I was saying the Lord's Prayer, thinking I would be crushed underneath these people (I don't move fast enough to get out of the way), I heard a woman and her husband saying words that didn't seem to fit the situation. As they were pushed into people, they took time to say, "Please excuse me. I'm so sorry."

The apology sounded strange. In an environment characterized by selfishness, these people demonstrated concern for their neighbors. The people whose forgiveness they sought always said, "That's quite all right; I understand." As people in the crowd heard the apologies, they began using the words as well. People apologized, confessing their offense, and proclaimed forgiveness. After a few minutes of this "confession and absolution," the mood of the crowd changed. It became more docile. In the face of this love, people who pushed and shoved felt shame. Even if their hearts weren't changed, their behavior was. People who might have begun to hate one another began to show sincere interest in one another. In a word, people were becoming friends.

That's what happens when people of God understand that their sinful condition causes them to behave inappropriately. They are quick to say, "Excuse me; please forgive me." We say it to God every day, and He always responds, "Go in peace, your sins are forgiven." We who have been justified by Jesus can pass on His forgiveness to others. We also can fearlessly confess our sins and ask forgiveness. Asking, receiving, and passing on forgiveness is catchy. It's like dropping a rock in a lake: The rings expand across the surface.

Church workers who know they are justified and free to say "Excuse me, I'm sorry" become leaven in the loaf of the congregation. That example encourages the entire church to behave graciously and with concern and love for one another. When church leaders have courage to confess their sins and ask forgiveness, the pushing and shoving stops.

Churches are like marriages. The healthiest ones are those in which you hear the words "I'm sorry" and "I forgive." May God enable all church workers to be polite, gracious people whose tongues easily and sincerely confess their sins, ask forgiveness, and pass the grace to others.

The Prayer: Lord, I want to lead Your people in ways that honor You. Enable me to confess my sins and to ask forgiveness from others. Then, O Lord, Your love shines through all of us. And, Father, make me quick to forgive those who sin against me. Grant this all for Jesus' sake. Amen.

~25~

The Word Still Becomes Flesh ... Really!

> At this the Jews began to grumble about Him because He said, "I am the bread that came down from heaven." They said, "Is this not Jesus, the son of Joseph, whose father and mother we know? How can He now say, 'I came down from heaven'?" *John 6:41–42*

A big challenge for church workers is their own humanity. Not that being human is something of which to be ashamed. What makes our humanity a problem is when we humans try to speak for God. A much-heard phrase directed at church workers is "Who does he think he is?" or "What gives her the right to tell us what to do?" This becomes discouraging. It's hard to lead people who refuse to accept leadership. A pastor was once told by the church council, "Reverend, we hired you, and we can fire you." The council didn't believe that God had sent this man to be their pastor. He was a "hired hand." People always have had trouble believing human beings can speak for God.

Even Jesus encountered people who had that problem. When He declared Himself to be the Bread of Life, His neighbors took offense. "He puts His robe on one arm at a time just like the rest of us. Where does He get off speaking for God?" His neighbors were so upset with His claim that they tried to throw Him off a cliff.

People will listen to our words and understand them as the Word of God when we live among them. Jesus didn't become defensive when people questioned His authority. He didn't stop teaching and healing because some people assumed His power came from the devil. He always was available, working even to the point of exhaustion. He never spoke an unkind word, though others directed many at Him. Jesus sacrificed Himself, even to the point of dying on the cross for those who questioned His authority. As He was nailed to the tree, He asked His Father to forgive His executioners.

Because we are baptized into Christ, this lifestyle is ours too. St. Paul confirms this in Ephesians 3:20–21 when he writes: "Now to Him who is able to do immeasurably more than all we ask or imagine, according to His power that is at work within us, to Him be glory in the church and in Christ Jesus throughout all generations, for ever and ever! Amen." Our humanity ceases to be a problem because Christ works within us despite our weaknesses. People see us forgiving others more often than would appear logical. People see us loving people who aren't particularly likable. A person without Christ can't do these things. People will be astounded at how we face life's problems with faith and confidence in our heavenly Father.

My orthopedic surgeon, a Buddhist, once told me that after 25 years of practice, he had learned how to identify which of his patients were Christian. He claims that non-Christians hate pain and become disgusted with him if he cannot immediately remove the pain. Christians, he declares, believe that pain may have a purpose. He said, "You Christians believe you can be friends with the pain and that it will somehow make you better." He's right. Jesus uses our weakness to show His strength.

Like our Lord, church workers accept their humanity and do not become discouraged when criticized. Instead of being discouraged, we rejoice as the Spirit of God molds us in the image of Jesus. From our weak bodies, people see faith, love, patience, hope, and a great God.

The Prayer: Dear God, strengthen me as I bring Your Word to the world. Keep rejection from discouraging me. Teach me to concentrate on imitating Christ every day so through my humanity, the love and power of Christ shines fervently. In His name. Amen.

~26~

Blessed by the Struggle

That night Jacob got up and took his two wives, his two maidservants and his eleven sons and crossed the ford of the Jabbok. After he had sent them across the stream, he sent over all his possessions. So Jacob was left alone, and a Man wrestled with him till daybreak. When the Man saw that He could not overpower him, He touched the socket of Jacob's hip so that his hip was wrenched as he wrestled with the Man. Then the Man said, "Let Me go, for it is daybreak." But Jacob replied, "I will not let You go unless You bless me."
Genesis 32:22–26

Generally, I sleep well. About the only time I have trouble sleeping is after we've had a congregational meeting that didn't go well. "Didn't go well" means that people wanted to take a direction that I didn't feel was good. In my early years of ministry, I became depressed about those types of meetings. Now I get excited about them.

This change of heart came after a careful reading of Genesis 32. Jacob is literally at the crossroad of his life. He wants to be reconciled to his brother, Esau. He is not sure that reconciliation is possible because he remembers the bad things he did to Esau. Jacob could understand if Esau wanted nothing to do with him, or worse, wanted to hurt him. He sends his family off to a safe place and sends gifts in Esau's direction. Jacob then goes to sleep.

If I were Jacob, I would have gone to sleep asking God to give me the "peace that passes all understanding" so I could sleep. That's not what God gives to Jacob. Instead of peace, God enters into a wrestling match with him. God does this because He knows it is the best way for Jacob to grow in faith.

Jacob could have tried to run from his resting place, but he didn't run. Instead, he was locked in the grip of God. Jacob felt God's breath warming the back of his neck. He felt God's strength measured against his own. Jacob knew he could never beat God, but he would hang on until God blessed him. Jacob got his blessing.

This story teaches us that when we struggle in our ministries, we're not struggling only with flesh and blood. Church workers are blessed to understand that the struggle about ministry direction isn't only with cantankerous Mr. Schmidt. They may be struggling with the Almighty who wants to bless them. God puts a hold on us to help us grow in Him. Knowing that we wrestle with God and not only our brothers and sisters, we focus our insight on ourselves instead of on the faults of others. That way we grow, or in the words of the text, God blesses us.

The blessing Jacob received was unusual. He received a limp. It was a tremendous blessing because the limp made it impossible for Jacob to think that he was sufficient by himself. Never again would Jacob play God and do destructive things like stealing a birthright.

In the morning, Jacob was tired, weak, humble, and overwhelmed by God's presence in his life. He was ready to make peace with his brother. May God allow us to struggle with Him daily. May that struggle bless us by making us tired, weak, humble, and overwhelmed by God's presence. May He make us ready to seek peace with our neighbors and brothers and sisters.

The Prayer: Dear Lord, in this world I shun pain and struggle. It is hard for me to believe that struggle and conflict can come from Your hand as a blessing. Open my eyes so I can focus on You. Give me the power to wrestle with You and thus be blessed. May that blessing enable me to be reconciled to others. In Jesus' name. Amen.

~27~

Overcoming Evil with Good

See that none of you repays evil for evil, but always
seek to do good to one another and to all.
1 Thessalonians 5:15 (NRSV)

A pastor friend of mine from another denomination
always amazed me with his enthusiasm for his work. His
enthusiasm was a by-product of his love for the people he
served. He spoke repeatedly of how blessed he was to serve
that congregation. Everything I heard about his ministry was
positive, so you can understand that I was almost as stunned
as he was when the congregation voted to release him.

My friend was hurt, confused, and angry. What dis-
turbed him most was that he couldn't get a clear reason for
the decision. After three futile days spent trying to get information, he cleaned out his office. With his books in his
apartment, he began to network with friends and judicato-
ry officials, looking for a place to serve.

It was about this time that his phone rang. It was the
president of his former congregation. The president reported that the senior pastor had become ill and wouldn't be
able to preach. They had contacted every retired minister in
the area, but no one was available to fill the pulpit. "In a
desperate measure," he said, "we decided to call you
because we knew you would be free this weekend." It took
all my friend's self-control not to give the man a severe
tongue-lashing. After a few awkward, silent moments, my
friend said, "Yes, I'll be happy to preach this weekend."

My friend began to work on the sermon, which he made sure reflected the love and forgiveness of Christ. When Sunday came, he preached a sermon grounded in the Gospel. He reassured the congregation that their future was safely in God's hands, but he made no reference to his termination. During that week, he had faced what appeared to be evil, but he trusted Jesus to help him overcome evil with good. Jesus gave him success.

He learned how successful he was about three years later. At that time, the senior minister at the time of his termination died unexpectedly. This former congregation extended a call to him. My friend is convinced the only reason it happened was the sermon he had preached three years before. The Spirit of God truly used it to change people's hearts—to overcome evil with good.

Church workers frequently have opportunity to overcome evil with good. Sometimes that opportunity comes too frequently. Regardless of how much evil we endure—unfair accusations, gossip, lies, inadequate compensation—we ask God to keep us strong, to keep us from surrendering to evil. We pray fervently that Jesus would give us gracious things to say and gracious things to do during difficult times. We know He will. He has promised that when we are called to give an account of our faith, we don't have to worry because God will give us the right words. We will not speak, but the Spirit of our Father will speak through us (Matthew 10:19–20).

Jesus will put words of love and forgiveness on our lips just as He did for my friend. Those words, authored by Jesus, will change people's hearts. A whole congregation learned a lesson about love, humility, and forgiveness because a baptized man of God preached love instead of vengeance. The same power, working through the Word to change individuals and congregations, is alive and well in our baptized hearts.

I don't care to have evil confront me. However, knowing that Jesus can strengthen me to overcome evil with good almost makes me want to bring it on. If dealing with evil can lead people to faith in Jesus or to a closer relationship with Him, then let the evil come. It will be overcome.

The Prayer: Lord Jesus, You faced evil every day of Your life. You always overcame evil with good. Your crucifixion and resurrection are clear witness to Your power to turn evil into good. Wherever evil enters my life, help me to respond with love and grace. In Jesus' name. Amen.

~28~

The Joy of Salvation

*Restore to me the joy of Your salvation, and uphold me
by Your generous spirit. Psalm 51:12 (NKJV)*

"Reverend, that's the first time in my life I went to a
wedding and could tell it wasn't a funeral." The speaker
went on to describe the church as being a bunch of people
"hoping to get to heaven on the length of their faces and
the strength of their arguments."

The proof of such a statement may be supported on
Sunday morning as we watch people approach or leave the
Lord's Table. Many squeeze their faces into a serious stare. It
appears they believe that what makes them a worthy commu-
nicant is their reverence, not their faith. Maybe it's true that in
the American church "many are called, and a few are frozen."

That's not the way God would have it. He wants His
people to demonstrate joy. Scripture offers no admonish-
ment to the shepherds and Wise Men who approached
Jesus with joy. No one silences Simeon or Anna when they
embrace the Messiah, Jesus. The Bible doesn't censure the
angels who rejoice in heaven over one sinner who is saved.
Therefore, it seems we have a tremendous instrument with
which to do our ministry—laughter.

We have been spared eternal punishment and have
been given eternal joy and a reason to laugh. Because Jesus
gave us life, it's all right to laugh in worship. I once opened
a ciborium full of hosts in front of an oscillating fan, which
sent 55 hosts scattering all over the chancel. The people
couldn't help laughing out loud. God was not mocked. We
just replenished our supply of hosts.

One time a young boy who was serving for the first time as an acolyte was told to pause and bow every time he passed the center of the altar. The boy did as he was instructed. The only problem was that he didn't bow toward the altar. He turned around and bowed toward the congregation as though he had just finished a performance. The congregation laughed and immediately bonded with the boy.

The congregation laughed when I told them about a retreat at which I fell out of a boat and had to negotiate with my staff before they pulled me in. The congregation laughed so long and so hard that passers-by stopped, walked to the open windows, and listened. Laughter attracts people. Our laughter stems from knowing that Jesus will take us to live with Him forever. We take Jesus very seriously and don't have to take ourselves seriously at all.

Let the world know the difference between a lecture and a worship service through the joy expressed. Show the world the difference between a stockholders' meeting and a congregational meeting through laughter and trust in God. Let every family who brings their children to a parochial school know their children are in an environment where happiness is allowed and encouraged through our eagerness to laugh and smile.

Pray daily that Jesus restores to all the joy of salvation and the gladness, joy, and laughter it brings. Pray for the power to make it obvious.

The Prayer: Lord, You have given me joy in Your presence. Let my joy be obvious to all, and may my joy, offered in this troubled world, lead people to You, the source of all joy. In Jesus' name. Amen.

~29~

Between a Rock and a Hard Place

Moses answered the people, "Do not be afraid. Stand firm and you will see the deliverance the LORD will bring you today. The Egyptians you see today you will never see again. The LORD will fight for you; you need only to be still." *Exodus 14:13–14*

There they were. The Egyptian army was breathing down their necks, and the Red Sea lay in front of them. They could turn around and fight the world's most powerful army or try to swim across the sea. They did neither because they knew they could not survive on their own. God would have to intervene and deliver them. God did intervene, and this story of deliverance is second only to Jesus' resurrection. Israel found itself between a rock and a hard place, and God took them to a high place.

This is good news for church workers. Although we're often not warned by those who train us for professional church work, church workers frequently find themselves between "Pharaoh's army" and the "Red Sea."

Maybe this sounds familiar. A teacher who has served a congregation for years begins to change. Love toward students is replaced with resentment. Kind, patient words of encouragement are replaced with screams, shouts, and threats. Rough handling has replaced reassuring pats on the head. This is a disaster waiting to happen. The principal and pastor meet to share the problem and to prayerfully determine what to do. When the teacher meets with the pastor and principal, she assures them that nothing is wrong except that she is teaching incorrigible children with difficult parents. The difficulties continue despite several meetings with the principal and a few with the pastor. The Board of Education is aware of the problem. After prayer, thought, and anguish, they decide not to renew the teacher's contract.

Once the news of the teacher's release is public, some people understand and are grateful for the decision. The teacher's family and closest friends are incensed. They criticize the leadership to anyone who will listen. Attitudes about church leaders begin to change as the teacher's supporters place these leaders' names and actions in a negative light.

This is the proverbial rock and a hard place for church workers. No one looks forward to such events. No one can avoid them, no matter how loving and caring they are. These experiences always cause pain and anxiety. Under such pressure, we, like the people of Israel, may ask, "Why did You bring us out here in public ministry? Wouldn't it be easier for us to be something else?"

In the midst of this pain and anxiety, professional church workers never can forget that they serve a God who knows about being between a rock and a hard place. Jesus Himself hung between the rock hard judgment of the world and the hard place of death. In that position, He also experienced the power of God. God reached in and raised up His Son, vindicating Him from the charges and accusations against Him.

In the midst of our rock and hard place, God does the same thing. He lifts His cross over our dilemma, and He brings life and deliverance. Jesus gives strength to leaders so they can put their reputations aside and do what is best for the church. Jesus gives strength to decision-makers so they can endure the second-guessing of others. Finally, Jesus will bring deliverance. People will in time see God's hand in the whole experience.

God in Christ has promised to deliver us from every dilemma. Therefore, we can be diligent in trying to fix situations in which God's people are being hurt. Placing the needs of the church above our own desire to be liked and respected is a wonderfully liberating experience.

People without Christ worry about situations because they have no idea how to handle their problems. They may resort to lying, manipulating, or running away. Those who are baptized into Christ know that Jesus will deliver us, so we need not concentrate on repercussions or ramifications. Instead, we can focus on actions that bless His Church.

The Prayer: O Lord, Your people always have found themselves between rocks and hard places. Every time they find themselves in these situations, You extend Your mighty hand and deliver them. Help me to recall how You delivered Your people of old so I might remain faithful to You. Grant this for Jesus' sake. Amen.

~ 30 ~

Cutting-Edge Ministry

> Yet more than ever believers were added to the Lord, great numbers of both men and women, so that they even carried out the sick into the streets, and laid them on cots and mats, in order that Peter's shadow might fall on some of them as he came by. *Acts 5:14–15 (NRSV)*

Cutting-edge ministry is an often-used phrase today. It becomes a goal to which people aspire. We want our Sunday school to be on the cutting-edge. We want our evangelism program to be on the cutting-edge. We want our worship program to be on the cutting-edge.

Hundreds of people have written hundreds of books and articles that tell church workers how to modernize and perfect their ministries. These writings tell what to do and what not to do to gather people into the church and school.

Our church has listened to these suggestions. Some we find helpful; some we find confusing and frightening. It is difficult to believe that the success or failure of a ministry could depend on a list of dos and don'ts or on a certain style of worship or youth ministry.

The New Testament comforts church workers who are concerned about what does and doesn't work. The New Testament makes it clear that what places a church on the cutting-edge is not worship style, parking space, or nurseries. The New Testament tells us that people are attracted when they see Jesus in a church.

Peter didn't have a worship facility in which to preach. He escaped the controversy over contemporary or traditional music. He didn't have a problem with child care. He never talked with a "Baby Boomer" or "Gen X-er." He did deal with Romans, Greeks, and Jews who practiced everything from hedonism to nationalism. He had none of the benefits of today's sociological studies, but his ministry was so successful that people tried to sit in his shadow, hoping for a blessing.

The people who waited for Peter's shadow to cover them did so not because of any special ministry strategy. They waited because Peter showed people Jesus through the Word when he preached good tidings to the afflicted. Peter showed people Jesus when he proclaimed liberty to people held captive. He showed people Jesus when he announced forgiveness of sins. He showed people Jesus when he brought comfort to mourners. He did these things with such power that people tried to make their way into his life, even if all they got was a shadow.

With all due respect to those who try to improve ministries through various strategies, what really makes ministries cutting-edge is God's Word at work through His servants. People will see Jesus when we love them, offer ministries and programs that meet their needs, and give up nonscriptural practices that people do not understand.

Many church leaders can't afford seminars and books that promote cutting-edge ministries. In fact, strategies and promotions are useless if God's Word and Jesus' love are absent in those who lead congregations. Therefore, as we plan and pray, ask the Spirit of God to help us grow in faith and show Jesus' love. When that happens, people will see God's Word in action and come to salvation.

The Prayer: Dear God, thank You for saving me through faith in Jesus Christ. I long to serve You as I bring Your saving Word to the world. Let Your Spirit so rule in my heart that I might show Jesus in all that I say and do. In Jesus' name. Amen.

~31~

Role Models

I appeal to you, then, be imitators of me.
1 Corinthians 4:16 (NRSV)

These words of St. Paul bothered me for a long time. They seemed arrogant. "Imitate me." I wondered if Paul always imitated Christ. There had to be moments when Paul didn't imitate Jesus. He even admits it in Romans 7. If this were true, how could he encourage others to follow his example?

Paul, like most Christians, wanted to be like Christ in everything he did and said. He knew that the growth of the church was dependent, in part, on how he modeled Jesus. Paul grew in the faith through the Word and through suffering and deliverance. His model inspired and guided the church.

Today's church needs models and guides too. By the grace of God, we are the models and guides that Christ chose to place before the church. Each of us should place on our mirrors this lesson: "Be imitators of Christ." Longing to be like Christ demonstrates that our will and God's will are one. It further demonstrates that He will bless our ministries because they are centered in Him.

The devil works hard to drive us away from Christ. He has much success in the area of stewardship. Some church workers, inadequately compensated for their work, refuse sacrificial giving. After all, they already give more time than anyone else and their insufficient income is a contribution of sorts.

St. Paul might commend us for giving our time. Yet there is another area for us to imitate Christ—the area of finances. The stewardship life of a congregation will never grow larger than the stewardship example set by its professional church workers. This can be a tremendous burden. Or it can be a tremendous privilege. Jesus would have us see it as a privilege.

The church I serve is like most churches—no one knows what others give. We don't publish contributions. I am amazed at how the members of our church know who gives firstfruit tithes and offerings to the Lord, especially if those people are church workers. Our people know a lot more about us then we could imagine.

Such knowledge is not bad. It is a privilege. We are called to imitate Christ. The attention people pay to us demonstrates how much they need us. They need us to model a Christlike life. Like St. Paul, we won't always be perfect witnesses to Christ, but God will make us more Christlike each day. May God so inspire us by His grace that we see the special privilege that He has given to us as models of Christ.

The Prayer: Dear Lord, thank You for giving me Your Son to model. I pray that You would make me a faithful witness to Jesus. Help me especially, O Lord, to show my church how to give of treasure in proportion to what You have given. In Jesus' name. Amen.

~ 32 ~

It's You and Me against the World!

"Do not be afraid, little flock, for your Father has been pleased to give you the kingdom." *Luke 12:32*

One of my favorite posters displays two cute Samoyed puppies sitting in a basket. The caption beneath reads: "It's you and me against the world, and frankly, I think we are going to get creamed!"

I believe this poster symbolizes how some church workers feel about their futures. Sometimes we feel small in the face of our challenges and troubles. It doesn't help that often we hear stories about church workers who were "creamed" by the people they served.

It is important for those of us who serve the church to realize that we can never be "creamed." That is, we cannot be brought to shame through malice or evil. There will be moments when church workers appear defeated, but these moments are snippets of time. If the world only saw Jesus on Good Friday, it would have to say He was brought to shame. If the world looks at the continuum from Friday to Sunday, it would see Jesus victorious.

Jesus knows that we will from time to time get "stuck on Good Friday." For some of us, Good Friday may seem to last for months or years. That's why Jesus assured us that it is the Father's good pleasure to give us the kingdom. God will make us triumphant. To paraphrase the poster, church workers can say to one another, "It's you and me against the world, and by the grace of God, we'll be victorious."

The church is not well-served by workers who expect to lose. The church is not well-served by cocky or arrogant workers. Church workers who go about their work declaring that "all things will work together for good for those who love God and are called according to His purposes" bring resurrection power to the people they serve.

Resurrection power brings confidence that enables congregations to grow and overcome obstacles. We want our witness to Jesus to shout that though we look as weak and helpless as puppies, in Christ we are more than strong. The Father has given us the kingdom. We can be confident as we live and work with the world's vagaries and difficulties. And confidence, like a cold, is contagious. May God make us all contagiously confident.

The Prayer: O Lord, the disciples of old locked themselves behind closed doors out of fear. Your Son came among them and showed proof of His victory. You have chosen to give me the kingdom, Father, and I thank You. Now may I, just like the disciples of old, grow in confidence because You are still present. In Jesus' name. Amen.

~33~

Competition and the Church

> John said to Him, "Teacher, we saw someone casting out demons in Your name, and we tried to stop him, because he was not following us." But Jesus said, "Do not stop him; for no one who does a deed of power in My name will be able soon afterward to speak evil of Me. Whoever is not against us is for us." *Mark 9:38–40 (NRSV)*

I always chuckle a little when I hear the scores from parochial school sporting events. Our Savior killed Christ the King 11–1. Prince of Peace fell to St. Paul 5–4, and Concordia humiliated St. John 22–0. The words don't ring true. Why would our Savior want to compete with Christ the King, aren't they the same person? Why would someone with the name "harmony" want to humiliate anyone, especially an evangelist as powerful as St. John?

On the surface, it sounds like a word game. The truth is competition always will be a problem for the church, and it will never have a legitimate place.

Americans have been taught that competition is good, which makes our lives as American Christians difficult. Jesus spoke directly to the issue of competition when the disciples explained how they had tried to protect His ministry. John reported that they saw a man casting out demons in Jesus' name. Because the man was not part of the group, they told him to stop. John was threatened by the competition; Jesus was above it. He told John to stop such insecure behavior and consider the growth of the kingdom—not who deserved the credit for the growth. He closed the subject by teaching that those who aren't against Him are for Him.

It's important for the church and its professional workers to understand Jesus' teaching. The preacher who approaches tasks from a nontraditional style and shepherds a growing church is not an enemy. The teacher who brings new activities and methodologies into a classroom and enjoys the adoration of parents is not an enemy. The neighboring congregation that is growing quickly deserves support and admiration, not scorn. We compete with no one but the devil.

Again Jesus makes that clear: The fields are ripe for harvest, but the laborers are few (Matthew 9:37). Therefore let us rejoice over the harvest that is being gathered rather than feel threatened by someone else's harvest. The harvest doesn't belong to us; it is the Lord's.

When the Spirit of Jesus frees us from self-centered competition with other Christians, we are free to learn from one another. Christians who join hands in service become a strong obstacle to sin as long as they don't sacrifice the Word. Jesus shows us the effectiveness of the Church and of church workers who resist competition when He prays in John 17 that the Church would be one, even as He and the Father are one. The purpose for that prayer is powerful. Jesus wants the Church to be united in His Word so the world may know His salvation. The key, of course, is total dependence on His inerrant, wholly sufficient Word.

For the sake of the world that Jesus died to save, let's put competition behind us and employ our strength to cooperate with brothers and sisters in Christ. May the day come soon when people hear that St. Paul supported Our Savior in its most recent evangelism drive. That Concordia congratulated St. John on its new building and its increase in worship attendance. That the youth groups from Prince of Peace and Christ the King joined hands to build a house for a homeless family.

May we always be known as the church that cooperates and never as the church that competes.

The Prayer: O Lord, You know my selfishness. Even in the church I compete with others for victories, new members, and praise. Rid Your church of such competition, God, by opening my ears to the Word of Jesus. Help me lovingly embrace all who are not against You. In Jesus' name. Amen.

~34~

The Power of the *Plunk*

Then the eyes of the blind shall be opened, and the ears of the deaf unstopped; then the lame shall leap like a deer, and the tongue of the speechless sing for joy. *Isaiah 35:5–6 (NRSV)*

Little things can be destructive. Scientists say that if you take a large rock and simply drip water on it—*plunk, plunk, plunk, plunk*—in time, the rock will break. One little drop of water, one little *plunk,* appears harmless; applied repeatedly, it brings disastrous consequences.

So it is with the way people relate to one another and to God. Although each individual complaint, criticism, unkind word, or injustice doesn't seem like much, each *plunk* carries catastrophic potential. The words and actions of those called into public ministry carry an even larger *plunk* than usual. People look to us with hope. They expect that Jesus enables us to do more than we could ever ask or think. He will. That brings new power to the *plunk*.

When the *plunk* is a word of kindness to a child experiencing a difficult day, the child begins to heal. When the *plunk* is a word of forgiveness to someone who has offended us, reconciliation begins. When the *plunk* is praise for a colleague, the encouragement builds commitment and enthusiasm.

The *plunks* of anger, resentment, and callousness come from the devil. The *plunks* of love, encouragement, appreciation, and kindness come from God. The *plunks* from God accomplish healing and progress. There is no such thing as a meaningless act of kindness or a harmless word of teasing. Acts of kindness and love by church workers build up people quickly. Acts of criticism and teasing by church workers tear down people quickly.

As church workers, we can celebrate the power of our speech and actions, power given by God. Therefore, we use our words and deeds to build up people just as Jesus has strengthened us. As we do this, we have the opportunity to see the power of the *plunk* right before our eyes. People begin to grow and heal and live under the power of the *plunk* offered in Jesus' name. We know the feeling. Jesus *plunks* us sinners with the salvation He earned on the cross.

The Prayer: Lord Jesus, You fill Your people with power. Help me use this power for good. May all that I say and do be a part of Your healing plan for others. In Your name. Amen.

~ 35 ~

Doing Our Part

"He who has ears to hear, let him hear." *Luke 14:35*

Some people have the "gift of gab." I was with one such person at a recent church meeting. This individual had a comment about most things and an opinion about everything. The meeting began to drag under his words. As the frustration level rose, the chairperson stood up and said, "Friend, the Lord has given you two ears and one mouth. I humbly submit that the work of this committee will go forward more efficiently if you were to use them in that ratio."

Jesus knew we would need to be reminded about the importance of listening. That's why He said, "He who has ears to hear, let him hear." Hearing and being heard are two requirements for effective living and church work. Jesus comes among His people to open sin-deafened ears. He does this by helping us hear our own voice.

A newly formed church choir had been receiving wonderful accolades from its grateful congregation. For some choir members, this praise suggested they had a superior ability, one that made the choir director unnecessary. Week after week, members of the choir would not listen to their parts. Instead, they improvised and "improved" on their parts. The end result was a disorganized sound and a frustrated director. He decided the only way to get the choir to stop behaving this way was to let them hear how they sounded. He taped the next service. When he replayed the tape, the choir felt hurt by what they heard. They didn't sound as good as they thought. Many, after hearing themselves as they really were, pledged never to sing again. The wise choir director suggested something less drastic. He said, "Why not listen to your part and do your best to sing it?" The choir listened, and the sound was magnificent.

Church workers can do the same thing. We can listen to how well our voice fits with God's "choir." When we are enamored with our own voice, Jesus would have us see how horrible that voice sounds as it attempts to blend with the voices of people with whom we work. It sounds even worse when it solos apart from God's will and His Word. He would have us "re-tune" our voice by using our ears. Our ears listen to His voice as He speaks through the Word and our coworkers. Then our voice is raised in love, and the result is beautiful harmony.

May the Lord enable us to remember that we have two ears and one mouth. May we use them for Jesus in that ratio.

The Prayer: Dear Lord, You always have been concerned that people hear Your voice. What often prevents me from hearing You is my desire to speak. Help me to place my voice under Your Lordship. Help me listen to the needs of others and to Your leading so when I speak, I bring Your love to others. In Jesus' name. Amen.

~36~

Which Great Commission?

"My prayer is not for them alone. I pray also for those who will believe in Me through their message, that all of them may be one, Father, just as You are in Me and I am in You. May they also be in Us so that the world may believe that You have sent Me." *John 17:20–21*

I've participated in several celebrations of our Lord's Great Commission. At these gatherings, we have learned how to share Jesus through special words or special questions. We've learned how to develop programs that encourage nonbelievers to visit and hear the Gospel. Most of these things work—people do come to our churches, and they do hear the Gospel.

When we receive new members into our congregation, I get nervous. My anxiety stems from their enthusiasm. Many believe they have truly found the "communion of saints." Then, after joining a Bible study group or serving on a committee, they run into something that shocks and scandalizes them—conflict.

Each new member God brings to the body of Christ needs to be prepared for the truth about congregations if they are to escape disappointment and disillusionment. The truth is that we are not perfect, and we do have conflicts and disagreements.

The devil loves these conflicts and disagreements. When the church fights, regardless of how "sacred" the issue, the world becomes less confident in our Gospel message. So what is the greatest commission that Jesus gave the church? Is it to "go," or is it to be "one"? I believe that we can "go" all we want, but if the body of Christ doesn't set itself apart from society, our efforts are greatly compromised. Therefore, I would suggest that church workers particularly emphasize "unity" in their ministries.

Unity is a gift from God. It comes through the mind of Christ, which has been given to the Church. Jesus enters our minds and enables us to see that our real enemy is not the teacher who teaches math differently. It isn't the preacher who has an unusual style, nor is it the church member who believes the congregation spends money the wrong way. These are brothers and sisters with whom we are called to be reconciled. The enemy is the devil who tries to make that reconciliation impossible.

Pastors, teachers, and parents have instructed children about the danger of peer pressure. We have worked hard to place children in environments where peer pressure is positive. May God make our churches, faculties, and staffs places where peer pressure is positive. By encouraging coworkers who are in conflict with others, we submit to our Lord's will for unity, which enables the church to grow.

Church workers can do several things to help grow the kingdom of God. Bible study, prayer, hard work, preparation, planning, and evaluation are things we can do to help the kingdom grow. In addition, kingdom work is only effective when we work as a team with Jesus as our Leader and the Word as our guide.

The Prayer: Dear Lord, our church has been going for You for years. Not all our "going" has resulted in growth. Your Word teaches that growth is difficult for the church when there is no unity. Make us one, Lord. Remove from all Your church workers self-righteousness, self-centeredness, and pride. Give us loving, servant hearts to embrace our coworkers and the people we serve. In His name. Amen.

~37 ~

Here He Comes

"You shall not give false testimony against your neighbor." *Exodus 20:16*

I have a ritual that takes place in the church and school parking lot. I watch parents gathering to speak with one another. Sometimes their conversations reflect true Christian fellowship. Other times these conversations please the devil because they violate the Eighth Commandment. When people enjoy Christian fellowship, they welcome me into their circle. When people gossip and see me coming, I read their lips. They say, "Uh oh, here he comes."

Initially, I was pleased to think my presence caused people to change their conversation. Then I discovered I hadn't changed anything. You see, instead of curtailing the gossip, these folks moved the location from the parking lot to the local coffee shop. I realized my presence could not change the hearts of those who wanted to gossip. Only Christ's presence can do that. This realization changed the way I dealt with those who enjoyed criticizing others. Instead of trying to identify them and "catch them in their crime," I loved them. I encouraged them to share their concerns directly with the people about whom they talked. I made every effort not to speak evil of them to anyone else, no matter how disappointed I was.

Is there too much gossip and backbiting at your place of service? Begin by asking Jesus to use you to stop it. He'll use you not as a police officer, but as an obedient foot-washer. Jesus will use you as an example of how to replace evil with good. Even better, He will use you as an example of one who forgives because God's forgiveness has personal meaning. Pray that your ministry results in such love that when people see you coming in their direction, even on the parking lot, they will say, "O good! Here he (or she) comes!"

The Prayer: Heavenly Father, gossip hurts. It hurts those who are the target, and it hurts You because Your love calls us away from such destructive behavior. Help me to love gossipers so they see Jesus in me, recognize their sin, feel His love and forgiveness, and have their hearts and minds changed. May they replace words of gossip with words of thanks and praise. In Jesus' name. Amen.

~38~

A Good Example

Philip said, "Lord, show us the Father and that will be enough for us." Jesus answered, "Don't you know Me, Philip, even after I have been among you such a long time? Anyone who has seen Me has seen the Father. How can you say, 'Show us the Father'?" John 14:8–9

My grandmother was 98 years old when she died. She was an amazing woman. She had lived through and raised a family during the Depression and two world wars. She was married to my grandfather for 65 years. Since his death, she lived by herself. She fixed her own meals, cleaned her own home, paid her own bills, and loved her Lord. She is my family hero.

I speak about my grandmother whenever I get the chance. Sometimes I'm afraid I speak of her in such glowing terms that I bore people. I think I even made one person mad. This person said, "You make it sound like your grandmother was God." I found that response sobering. After what seemed like an eternity, I responded, "No, my grandmother was not God, but she was an excellent example of Jesus' love living in believers."

When I told my grandmother that story, she began to cry. Putting my arms around her, I said, "Grandma, I didn't mean to make you sad. I'm sorry!"

"I'm not sad," she said. "I'm astonished! You see, if that's true, then all my prayers have been answered. All I've ever wanted to do with my life is to be an example of Jesus to people."

My grandmother's prayers were answered. She spent a lifetime showing people Jesus. Isn't it amazing that God makes people so effective? This is the same effectiveness God has planned for every professional church worker. God strengthens each of us to live and serve as living examples of His love for us in Jesus Christ. This sounds like a lofty goal, but by the power of the Word working through the Spirit, it is possible.

The world, just like Philip, wants to see God. After all, seeing is believing! People see God first through His Word, then through you and me. Those who live in this century have seen tremendous feats of power and intelligence, such as space travel and the eradication of smallpox. It's difficult for them, however, to see God's hand in things that have become so ordinary. When the person whose automobile you hit doesn't sue you and instead shows concern for your well-being, you are amazed. When you forgive someone and use that experience to improve your relationship, the person never forgets it. Acts of love and service, not acts of power and might, show people the Gospel's impact on daily life.

People like us are in a unique and wonderful position. We can do what even medical science and technology cannot do—we can be models of Jesus' love and evidence of a God who cares for His people. We demonstrate His existence to the communities in which we live and serve by showing them the forgiveness and faithfulness we have received from God.

You may believe that waiting 20 minutes with a child whose parents forgot him at school is nothing, but in God's plan you are a living example of Jesus. You may think that forgiving the mother who criticized you at the last parent-teacher meeting is nothing, but you were a mirror of God's forgiveness. Thanking the parishioner who criticizes your sermon may seem inconsequential, but to the people who witness your grace, it's proof that Jesus lives in you.

Wouldn't it be great if, when our service ends, people remember us not for our accomplishments, but for the many ways God's love shines through us? May the Lord grant this gift to us all.

The Prayer: Father in heaven, when people look for You, send them to me. Let Your Spirit so shape and mold me that my life is characterized by a love and service that could only come from You. In Jesus' name. Amen.

~39~

How Many Days until School Is. Out?

I am not saying this because I am in need, for I have learned to be content whatever the circumstances. I know what it is to be in need, and I know what it is to have plenty. I have learned the secret of being content in any and every situation, whether well-fed or hungry, whether living in plenty or in want. Philippians 4:11–12

A dear partner in ministry has an uncanny awareness of his calendar. It's not that he knows what he's doing every evening until the end of the year. It's more like he knows how many days remain until the next school vacation. After the first day of school, he proudly announces that the faculty only has 168 more days of instruction. If you want to know how many days remain until Christmas or Easter break, ask my friend. He knows.

Although his attention to the calendar is humorous, sometimes I wonder if it doesn't betray dissatisfaction with his work. I wonder why he counts the days until vacations if he enjoys what he does? If the truth were known, I'm sure my friend is not the only church worker who isn't content. Many church workers spend the day thinking about where they would rather be instead of what they are actually doing.

This preoccupation with something other than the present task doesn't mean people lack dedication. It means the devil is alive and tempting productive church workers.

Helping God's people become dissatisfied has been the *modus operandi* of the devil since the Garden of Eden. He wanted Adam and Eve to "count the days" that they hadn't been permitted to eat the forbidden fruit rather than concentrate on other blessings. Just as such temptation worked on Adam and Eve, it works on us. And that's not good for the people we serve.

When church workers focus on "what they don't have" and on "where they aren't," the people they serve suffer. It's hard to be loving to people when you don't love where you are and what you are doing. When we find ourselves "counting the days" until the next break, the words of St. Paul speak to us: "I have learned to be content in any and every situation."

Those words sound strange coming from Paul. His entire ministry was full of trouble, including persecution. If anyone had a right to number the days until the next "break," it was him. But Paul does no such thing. He is content.

Paul has no trouble being content because he is aware of what he deserves from God. He routinely refers to himself as the "least of the apostles." He considers himself the least because he once persecuted the church. Paul knows that you can't complain about hunger and imprisonment when you know you could be suffering the pangs of hell!

We are in the same position St. Paul was in during his life. Without Christ, we are God's enemies. We deserve nothing except suffering and death. Because we sin against God daily, we don't deserve to look for days off or for places to serve where the grass is greener. We are simply grateful that God has chosen us for salvation and for service.

Paul also could be content because he learned that God pours meaning and purpose into every experience. To us it may seem like just another first day of school. To God, that first day may be the first day of life in Christ for a student. To us it may seem like just another busy Advent. To God, that Advent season is another opportunity for the congregation to grow in faith through a focus on His Word.

Every day that we serve God accomplishes something, even if we don't see it or understand it. That makes every day an epic day filled with power and grace. Knowing that God will bless our efforts with the fruit of faith makes us the kind of people who count our days—until our next chance to serve in Jesus' name.

The Prayer: Almighty and most gracious God, You have blessed all my days with food and shelter, with health and friends, with hope, and with effectiveness. Help me to thank You always for calling me into Your service. Teach me to rejoice and be content with my lifestyle. In Jesus' name. Amen.

~40~

That Thing Doesn't Have a Chance

"Truly I tell you, if you say to this mountain 'Be taken up and thrown into the sea,' and if you do not doubt in your heart, but believe that what you say will come to pass, it will be done for you." *Mark 11:23 (NRSV)*

The poor fellow's hands were shaking as though they were the epicenter of an earthquake. He couldn't keep his eyes or his mind on any one thing. He was scared. He had learned the day before that he was suffering from stomach cancer. A huge tumor had grown inside his body. The future was definitely in question for this 59-year-old man.

Every person in our church was praying for him. His Christian friends throughout the nation and world were praying for him. The night before the surgery, he and I prayed together. I held his hand, looked him in the eye, and said, "Jim, I feel sorry for that tumor. With God on your side, it doesn't have a chance!"

The surgery was an incredible success. Jim had a long, slow recovery. Now, years after the surgery, he has returned fully to his life and work. We reminisced about the illness, and Jim said, "You know, Pastor, you said a lot of wonderful things while I was fighting this disease, but the one thing I remember is that you felt bad for the tumor. Although it caught me by surprise, it was the truth. Now, no matter what happens in our family, we find ourselves using that phrase. That anger I'm feeling doesn't have a chance, God will help me handle it. That fear I feel doesn't have a chance, God will help me deal with it. That doubt I feel doesn't have a chance, God will help me overcome it."

That's what Jesus meant when He talked about faith that could move mountains. God's power is so great that nothing, not mountains or cancer, can stop us or separate us from His love. Jim certainly could have died from his cancer, but the tumor still didn't have a chance. If Jim had died, Jesus would have taken Jim to heaven. The deadly tumor would have been mocked.

Nothing can defeat the people of God. The empty cross and tomb and the Baptism that joins us to Jesus witness to this fact. Each of us can face troubles and challenges declaring, "They don't have a chance." That trouble that threatens your marriage—in Jesus, it doesn't have a chance. That child who threatens the peace and tranquillity of your classroom—in Jesus, he or she doesn't stand a chance. That sense of being unappreciated—in Jesus, it doesn't stand a chance of compromising your effectiveness. As servants of the most high and powerful God, notify the mountains that you're coming, armed with God's Word and His will.

The Prayer: Lord, Your death and resurrection has given me confidence for living. Help me face troubles and challenges remembering that no mountain is so big that You can't drown it in the middle of the sea. In Your name. Amen

~41~

The Church: A Great Place to Work

> Now we ask you, brothers, to respect those who work hard among you, who are over you in the Lord and who admonish you. Hold them in the highest regard in love because of their work. Live in peace with each other. *1 Thessalonians 5:12–13*

The word swept through campus like wildfire. The school secretary had resigned. Several people speculated as to why she had resigned. Some said it was the poor pay. Others said she wanted to spend more time with her family. A few said someone in the church had hurt her feelings. No one knew why she had resigned, except me. With a tissue in each hand wildly wiping away tears, she had repeated over and over again, " I just can't take this anymore."

The "this" to which she referred was the behavior of professional church workers. She told story after story of teachers using the school office as a place to make fun of the pastor or principal. She talked about how the youth worker tried to get people to "take sides" against those she didn't appreciate. She talked about how people couldn't stand prosperity. When something good happened, such as the church's purchase of property, the charge was made that "the church gets anything it wants, but the school and the youth program get nothing." Such talk depressed her and everyone else who heard it.

This behavior was so foreign to her understanding of how Christians were to live and work that it caused a crisis of faith. "Pastor, if I don't quit this job, I may become an unbeliever!" How tragic.

This and thousands of similar stories are the reason St. Paul told the church in Thessalonica: "Respect those who work hard among you, who are over you in the Lord and who admonish you. Hold them in the highest regard in love because of their work. Live in peace with each other." Paul's words are predicated on his understanding that people are by nature sinful and unclean. He knows that sometimes people don't love and admire one another, even in the church. He is aware, even from personal experience, that on a human level church workers don't always get along. Because of this, he appeals to a higher calling. St. Paul reminds us that those whom God has placed into public church work represent Him to the world. Therefore, they deserve honor and respect.

Some of us may think these words place an impossible demand on us. We may be convinced that some people are so offensive that we could never respect them. Such a position demonstrates the truth of our common confession that we are by nature sinful and unclean. Confess such enmity between church workers. Ask forgiveness and grant it to one another. Ask Christ to win the day through reconciliation of all involved.

Reconciliation will do more than provide church workers a peaceful workplace or prevent the resignation of church secretaries. Reconciliation will prevent others from stumbling, especially the "little ones" about whom Jesus was so concerned. Jesus was clear about what should happen to those who cause children to sin: "But if anyone causes one of these little ones who believe in Me to sin, it would be better for him to have a large millstone hung around his neck and to be drowned in the depths of the sea" (Matthew 18:6). Don't fear this sentence, instead cling to the love and grace Jesus makes available to everyone, especially to those who serve Him publicly.

No human in the world was more unappreciated, criticized, talked about, hurt, threatened, and persecuted than Jesus. Still He asked God to forgive those who had placed Him on the cross. He desired reconciliation, not revenge.

If you find yourself in conflict, look at three faces. First, look at Jesus' face. In that face, you will find unconditional love for everyone involved. In that face, you will find love for the whole world, a world He longs to have saved. Looking into the face of Jesus melts rage. Next, look into your face. Look for pride and self-centeredness. When you see your face filled with sin, realize that God sees your face covered by Jesus' righteousness. Jesus has removed the ugliness of sin. Last, look into the face of the person with whom you are angry. That person is beloved of God. That person is called by God. That person is forgiven by God.

In the name of Jesus and for the sake of the people we serve, may we always love, respect, and appreciate one another.

The Prayer: Lord, I love Your little ones, and I have no desire to cause them to sin. For that reason, I ask You to allow Christian workers everywhere, especially in our church, to love one another. Let none of us rest, O Lord, until we've worked for, encouraged, and realized unity. In Jesus' name and for His sake. Amen.

~42~

Acceptable Work

"His master replied, 'Well done, good and faithful servant! You have been faithful with a few things; I will put you in charge of many things. Come and share your master's happiness!' " *Matthew 25:23*

In this story, the man for whom the servant worked patted him on the back and told him he was doing a great job. It feels good when those for whom we work appreciate us.

Being appreciated may be more common when you work for only one person. That's often not the case with church workers. For some, it must seem like they have hundreds of bosses. Each boss has opinions and expectations. Sometimes those opinions and expectations conflict. In the same congregation, some praise us for the amount of homework we assign and others criticize us for the same thing. Some people think the church should grow, and they have little patience for leaders who don't preside over a growing congregation. Others see no need for the church to grow, and they aren't willing to support projects that might attract newcomers.

Some church workers could hear 200 compliments and one criticism and forget the praise and remember only the criticism. That may be the way we are, but that's not the way God wants us to be.

People who focus on negative comments risk losing their self-confidence, if not their joy. Creativity can suffer, and we can lose the courage required to lead God's people.

Consistent criticism can cause us to believe that God is calling us to a new place, even if we've only been in our present spot for a short time.

When criticism threatens our effectiveness or joy in ministry, we can recall for whom we actually work. We work for the Almighty, who, as part of His divine plan to spread the Gospel, has sent us to this place to serve Him. Although it's nice to hear praise, it is unnecessary and can be dangerous, particularly when it motivates the decisions we make and the services we offer.

It is far better for church workers to hear the evaluation of our work offered by our heavenly Father. Matthew says it best, as we read in today's Scripture passage. The One for whom we work accepts our service. Our service is never perfect, but God accepts it by His grace. He fills up what we leave empty. God would have us hear His Word of affirmation daily, which enables us to remain creative, bold, excited, and satisfied with the glorious work to which He has called us.

Each believer will, when they live with God in glory, hear these words: "Well done, you good and faithful servant." But God wants us to know that He says it everyday. "In My Son you did a fine job yesterday. In My Son, you'll do a fine job again today." Know that the pat on your back isn't just from a supportive coworker, it's from the Almighty.

The Prayer: Lord, thanks for Your support. When others criticize me and make me wonder whether I am fit for service, remind me that You called me to this work and, that by Your grace, my service is well done. In Jesus' name. Amen.

~43~

Reformers or Protesters?

"Master," said John, "we saw a man driving out demons in Your name and we tried to stop him, because he is not one of us." "Do not stop him," Jesus said, "for whoever is not against you is for you." *Luke 9:49–50*

At 11 years old, I attended my first Boy Scout weekend camp out. When Sunday came, the scoutmaster announced that religious services would be offered. He said that Catholic scouts would attend mass in the cafeteria, while Protestants would have a service in the campfire area. I waited for more, but he had no additional announcements. I asked, "Where do the Lutherans meet?"

He looked at me strangely and said, "Son, you're a Protestant."

I objected. "No, sir. I'm a Lutheran."

"Believe me, son, you're a Protestant," he said.

That experience confused me. I thought that Lutherans were the church of the Reformation, not the Protest. My training in Lutheran elementary school emphasized that Martin Luther wasn't interested in forming a new church, but in reforming the old one. I always have understood those words to describe the mission of Lutherans today—we are not to be against things, but we are to help people better understand God's Word.

Over the years, it seems like some Lutherans have lost sight of reforming and have embraced protesting. This makes a huge difference in how we go about our work. Protestants, by definition, have to be against something. They need to find things to be against to maintain their existence. The disciples in our Bible reading were good protesters. They found a man doing a wonderful thing, but because he.didn't meet their qualifications for ministry, they silenced him.

Jesus, on the other hand, is the consummate reformer. He sees that the man in question is doing useful work. He also sees the disciples have missed the point. They have demonstrated selfish pride about their relationship with Jesus. They want no one else to know the joy of service in Jesus' name. Jesus could have declared them unfit for service in His kingdom. Certainly, they had broken at least the First Commandment, maybe even the Eighth. But Jesus does not remove them from service. He chooses instead to reform them, and He does so through His Word.

As professional church workers, we are first and foremost reformers. Jesus daily reforms us from sin and doubt. Jesus would have us daily approach the people we serve as "works in progress"—people with whom God is not finished. We lovingly can speak God's Word to them and watch God bring them to new levels of faith.

A delegate attending the first session of a church convention said, "Now I know what we are against as a church. I hope in the next few days to find out what we are for." As we go about our work as servants of the most high God, we can make it our business to let people know what we are for. I think that's how the Church of the Reformation should go about its work.

The Prayer: Lord Jesus, as You corrected Your disciples who protested the good work of another, so correct me when I find fault in others. Truly make me an effective reformer who loves those You died to save. Make me anxious to guide others through Your Word. In Your name. Amen.

~44~

Giving It All Up for God

Then God said, "Take your son, your only son, Isaac, whom you love, and go to the region of Moriah. Sacrifice him there as a burnt offering on one of the mountains I will tell you about." *Genesis 22:2*

There are some who claim that God can be mean. The story of Abraham and Isaac might seem to prove that point. In this story, God asks Abraham to sacrifice his son. Abraham had waited a long time to have this son. The boy was a sign of God's promise. God's command must have shaken Abraham. He might have wondered if this could be the same God who had called him to be His own years ago. The sacrifice of a child was an aberration. How could God require this? Indeed, it seemed that God was being mean.

I felt that my parents were mean every time they punished me. In retrospect, I know they weren't mean. They were showing great love for me. It was the same between Abraham and God. God knew that Abraham would face many challenges. Life would not be easy. For these reasons, God wanted Abraham to trust Him, the promise maker, not the physical evidence of the promise. So God told Abraham to sacrifice Isaac. There could be no greater demonstration of love and faith than to sacrifice the "sign" of the promise.

God still treats His people the same way. Thanks be to God that He does. We, too, are tempted to put our faith in the sign of God's promises rather than in God Himself. We concentrate on the results of our faith rather than the walk of faith.

Church workers who need to see "signs" of God's presence in their ministry subject themselves to disappointment and disillusionment, particularly if they think the adulation of others is one of these signs. Had Jesus determined the success or failure of His ministry based on the love and acceptance of others, He would have declared Himself a failure. The "sign" that ultimately vindicated Jesus was His resurrection. It is the same for us. The "sign" that we are about "our Father's business" is the resurrection. Are people being regenerated in faith? Are families being reconciled around the love of Christ? Are people who never had time for God now receiving the Gospel with thanksgiving? Those are the signs on which we can focus.

To reach effectiveness in how we teach and live the Word, we may be called to sacrifice things previously precious to us. Sacrificing these "signs" of the kingdom, when God asks us to do so, demonstrates that He lives in us and our hearts are ruled by His love.

A study done by one church in Minnesota endeavored to discover how non-Christians perceive the church. The study revealed that the church exists to care for itself and is primarily concerned about receiving money from its members. Non-Christians perceived the church as unwilling to make sacrifices for God. It is our goal to see that this perception of the church changes.

May each of us take an inventory of our "Isaacs." Are there things that we can sacrifice because we depend on God for the present and the future? Can we conduct our lives and ministries in ways that make it clear we are willing to offer up anything for God if He should ask us to do so?

Abraham's willingness to sacrifice Isaac is a story that

has strengthened the faith of people for centuries. May God grant us the willingness and ability to make the same sacrifices so we may be people whose stories strengthen faith for years to come, as well.

The Prayer: Dear God, sometimes I place my faith and trust in the things of my ministry—schedules, traditions, beloved hymns, and the like. Move me to sacrifice these things if they ever get in the way of my service to people with the Gospel. In Jesus' name. Amen.

~45 ~

Envy and Jealousy in the Church

On the next Sabbath almost the whole city gathered to hear the word of the Lord. When the Jews saw the crowds, they were filled with jealousy and talked abusively against what Paul was saying. *Acts 13:44–45*

A church in the community I serve is growing rapidly. Hundreds of people are baptized each year. They have a youth ministry that attracts children from homes that haven't committed to any church. Our neighborhood sees this church as an exciting place that shows the best Christianity has to offer. You would think every Christian would rejoice in the accomplishments of this congregation. That's not the case. While some applaud the efforts and thank God for this church, others criticize. Those who criticize claim that this church has forsaken its roots.

I visited this church. I saw things I had never seen before. Singing "All Hail the Power of Jesus' Name" to a steel drum band is something I had never done, but it was effective. I watched and listened carefully. Although there were many innovations, the congregation confessed sins, both Law and Gospel were clearly preached, Scripture was read, and the Sacraments were administered rightly.

After visiting the church, I decided the criticism came not because of theological shortcomings, but because of jealousy on the part of congregations that hadn't enjoyed such growth. This isn't surprising. People have been jealous of those Jesus has used to gather people into the kingdom since the beginning. People were jealous and envious of Jesus too.

Envy is a sin. It suggests that God has made a mistake in the way He has distributed His gifts. If God had any real sense, He would give us more—more members, more money, more fun—at least as much as He has given to our thriving neighbors. Envy can destroy relationships anywhere, but it can do serious harm in the church.

Even 20th-century pagans know envy comes from self-centered people. When pagans hear of envy and jealousy among those supposedly on the "same side," they question both the transforming power of God and His very existence. Envy and jealousy among church workers are tools in the devil's hand that close ears and hearts to the Gospel. Envy and jealousy are sins of which to ask forgiveness. May God grant us the strength to repent. May He renew our lives.

God doesn't just remove the envy and jealousy from our hearts. He calls us to celebrate the success of our sister congregations. When Christians acknowledge success by others in ministry, the world sees that a peculiar Spirit lives in the hearts of Christians. It is the Holy Spirit.

It was the Holy Spirit who filled the heart of an imprisoned St. Paul. Upon hearing that others under suspicion were preaching the Gospel while he sat in jail, Paul said, "But what does it matter? The important thing is that in every way, whether from false motives or true, Christ is preached. And because of this I rejoice" (Philippians 1:18). These words demonstrate that Paul was not in ministry for his own ego, but for the sake of Jesus and the world.

That same Spirit lives in each of us today. He helps us demonstrate the difference Jesus made in our lives, freeing us from the tyranny of ego, as we honor God by praising what He accomplishes through others. The world will see this selflessness and know that it comes from God.

Most of us probably winced when our parents reminded us, "If you don't have anything good to say, don't say anything at all." Turn that thought inside out. If we have nothing good to say, ask God to help us see the good He sends through the situation.

The Prayer: Lord, it is true that the center of sin is "I." My ego can be bruised and I can feel threatened by the success of others. May Your Spirit so embrace me that I can leave my ego behind, rejoice in the success of others for Your kingdom's sake, and further place myself at Your disposal. In Jesus' name. Amen.

～46～

Giving Up a Dangerous Habit

"Do not judge, or you too will be judged. For in the same way you judge others, you will be judged, and with the measure you use, it will be measured to you. Why do you look at the speck of sawdust in your brother's eye and pay no attention to the plank in your own eye?" Matthew 7:1–3

We repeatedly hear about dangerous habits. While smoking heads the list, other dangers are drinking, poor eating, driving without seat belts, and living a sedentary lifestyle. Truly these are habits that need to be broken because each of them is capable of breaking us. In church work, there is another dangerous habit. It is the habit of judging others.

When we judge others, we are always wrong. We can't see into the mind and heart of a person whom we call before our "bench" to answer charges. When the prophet Isaiah identified a list of characteristics that will identify the Messiah, he included these words: "He will not judge by what He sees with His eyes, or decide by what He hears with His ears; but with righteousness He will judge the needy, with justice He will give decisions for the poor of the earth" (Isaiah 11:3–4). Our perfect Messiah will not judge by what He sees or hears, as we do. He will judge with His righteous heart, a heart we lost in the fall.

Once there was a young man who had difficulty in school. He had trouble reading and writing. He had trouble paying attention in class. This boy's teachers suspected that he had some special challenges. The parents were patient with the boy, choosing to work with him at home. He improved dramatically. Today we know this "stupid" boy as Albert Einstein. You have to wonder how his teachers felt when Einstein tremendously expanded scientific knowledge.

Christian church workers don't need to judge. It is, if you will, against our religion. We believe that God's power is so great that He can change any person at any time. Sauls become Pauls, doubters become believers, and fearful Peters boldly preach. God didn't judge these people and condemn them to remain stuck forever in their shortcomings. He calls us to treat others in the same way.

The lives of the people we serve and those who serve with us are daily filtered through the cross of our Lord Jesus Christ. The old goes away; the new comes forth. To judge them is to put limits on God. There is no place for such postures in God's kingdom. That's why God's Word encourages us to pay more attention to the plank in our own eye than the speck in our neighbor's eye.

As church workers, we can focus our attention on the cross of Jesus who took away the sins of the world. This will transform us to think and speak well of everyone we work for and with. It will give us time to concentrate on our own faith walk.

The Prayer: Lord, give me an abundance of Your grace so I may live like my Messiah and not judge by what my eyes see or by what my ears hear. Instead, remove the planks that fill my eyes. Grant this, O Lord, for Your kingdom's sake. Amen.

~47~

Thank You, God, That I'm a Married Church Worker

The man said, "This is now bone of my bones and flesh of my flesh; she shall be called 'woman,' for she was taken out of man." For this reason a man will leave his father and mother and be united to his wife, and they will become one flesh. *Genesis 2:23–24*

With these words, God announced that He had a plan for giving people a certain kind of help in life—help through companionship. Adam needed help. God had placed him in a beautiful world, but he was missing something. There was no one to share the beauty or the pleasures of godly work. God, out of His love, gave Adam what he needed—a helper. Their union made it possible to deal creatively with the lives God had given them.

The same thing happens among those of us who work in the church. From time to time, we meet church workers who are in wonderful situations. Their churches love and cherish them. Their ministries are well-received. The Holy Spirit uses them to nurture the faith of others. However, there may be little joy deep in their hearts. They are in a situation similar to Adam's. You can't thrive when you are alone. In His goodness, God provides helpers. Then life and ministry really change.

I am a husband and the father of four children. I am also the pastor of a large congregation. I love my wife. I love my children. I love my congregation. But sometimes my calendar reads like this:

6:30 A.M.: Take Rebecca to high school

7:30 A.M.: Take Tim and Naomi to elementary school

8:15 A.M.: Teach eighth-grade religion

9:30 A.M.: Counseling appointments begin

12:45 P.M.: Lunch with Chris (my wife), bring worship schedule for next year so she can work on music

2:15 P.M.: Pick up Naomi from school

3 P.M.: Bible class at Leisure World

4:30 P.M.: Pick up Tim from football practice

5:30 P.M.: Marriage counseling appointment

6:30 P.M.: Dinner

7 P.M.: Building committee meeting (explain to daughter that you can't make the mandatory parents' meeting for volleyball members—feel guilty during meeting)

11:30 P.M.: Return home, sort mail, take shower.

On days like this, I tend to think Roman Catholics have it right—celibacy is the way to go for church workers.

Married church workers have a wonderful blessing from God. But as the sign says, "Lord, give me the strength to withstand my blessings!" Married church workers face many challenges. They have at least two full-time jobs. They need to be creative to meet all the obligations. They also need help from others, though asking for help may be difficult. They can trust that God will continue His faithfulness. From personal experience, I can declare that He always does.

Married church workers also can avoid bemoaning the demands of family living. As married church workers, God gave us more blessings than challenges. How wonderful to have a spouse with whom you can pray every night! How encouraging to lift up together before the Lord your children. What a wonderful blessing to hear your child sing "Jesus Loves Me" for the first time! Married church workers are blessed repeatedly by their spouses and children. Most of that blessing comes down to one wonderful fact—the married church worker has a God-given helper.

Not every church worker has a spouse or children who understand ministry and the frustrations that accompany it. If we begin to feel married and alone, review the blessings our families bring to our lives. They are bone of our bone and flesh of our flesh. As we are reminded how clearly we are blessed through our families, ask God to help us enter the church and the world and bless others.

The Prayer: Dear Lord, thank You for the grace given to me through my spouse and my family. Help me always to cherish my family and take strength from them. Give me strength to accomplish all the tasks required of me. Help me to accept the help Your people offer. I ask this in Jesus' name. Amen.

~48~

Thank You, God, That I'm a Single Church Worker

I would like you to be free from concern. An unmarried man is concerned about the Lord's affairs—how he can please the Lord. But a married man is concerned about the affairs of this world—how he can please his wife—and his interests are divided. An unmarried woman or virgin is concerned about the Lord's affairs: Her aim is to be devoted to the Lord in both body and spirit. But a married woman is concerned about the affairs of this world—how she can please her husband. 1 Corinthians 7:32–34

We all have things that frustrate us. One thing that frustrates me is people who believe their calling is to be a matchmaker. I have seen them work hard to find a vicar a wife before he learns how to preach. I have witnessed them bombard a single teacher with the names of single sons, nephews, brothers, and friends. They are absolutely sure these two people will be a match made in heaven.

Matchmakers bother me not only because they impose their will on other people, but also because they may be imposing their will on God. I'm not sure why, but some church members believe that the only effective church worker is a married one. Nothing could be further from the truth.

Scripture is clear. God established ways for people to live. One of those ways is marriage, but another way is to be single. In fact, the ability to live by yourself is a spiritual gift. Those who have this gift find meaning and purpose in life through the work they offer to God. They don't feel they are missing anything. St. Paul affirms this lifestyle by adopting it himself. He thanks God for the freedom this lifestyle offers to be completely about the work of the Gospel.

Not a single word in the New Testament refers to St. Paul's need for a wife. No one says that Paul would make someone a great husband and that we need to find the right girl for him. And Scripture does not give the impression that Paul lived a less than happy and satisfied life.

God's Word has something to teach those who are single and those who think that "singleness" is less than a complete lifestyle. If you are a single church worker, Scripture would have you thank God for the privilege. The Bible suggests that you can accomplish things that married church workers might not accomplish. The Bible also wants you to know that you are a "whole person"—you lack nothing in God's eyes.

God invites you to feel good about your lifestyle. If you feel that you want to be married, that's fine. But God would have you marry not because you think you must marry to be a complete person or to be a complete church worker, but because you simply want to marry.

Those who would be matchmakers should understand that sometimes matchmaking flies in the face of God's will. Instead of imposing marital hopes on people, let God be God. Introduce people to each other to add to their stock of friends. If people we have introduced fall in love and marry, then, as the marriage liturgy says, "Blessed be God the

Father, the Son, and the Holy Spirit, now and forever." God deserves the credit.

It is appropriate for single church workers to proclaim, "Thank You, God, that I'm a single church worker." Whether married or single, Jesus is the Savior of all. He loves all people the same, and He blesses their work equally.

The Prayer: Lord Jesus, You equip people for godly lifestyles. Thank You for equipping me to serve You as a single person. Help Your Church to recognize Your hand and direction in my life. Continue to bless the work I undertake for You. In Jesus' name. Amen.

~49~

Hearing the Truth in Love

My child, be attentive to My words; incline your ear to
My sayings. Do not let them escape from your sight;
keep them within your heart. For they are life to those
who find them, and healing to all their flesh. *Proverbs
4:20–22 (NRSV)*

The congregation was growing steadily, though not by
leaps and bounds. As more people came to church, members
noticed that worship services took more time. Worship services lasted one hour and 20 minutes because of announcements, choir selections, and Holy Communion. This inter-
fered with Sunday school. A solution had to be found.

The elders of the church suggested changes in the distribution of Holy Communion. They were convinced that
continuous distribution would solve the problem. When
they announced the change, most members agreed with it.
Some didn't appreciate the change. A special congregational
meeting was called to discuss the issue. During that meeting,
one man said, "Pastor, we could save 10 minutes if you cut
the length of your sermons in half."

The pastor couldn't believe what he heard. How could
people even suggest that preaching of the Word should be
taken so lightly? What could be more important than to hear
faithful preaching of the Bible that rightly divided Law and
Gospel? The pastor took this suggestion personally and
became angry at the man who offered it. During the
10,000th repetition of those words in his mind, the pastor
realized the man didn't want to offend him. Instead, he was
trying to solve the problem. Looked at positively, the man

seemed confident that the pastor could preach for 10 minutes and still feed the congregation spiritually. The pastor decided to try the man's suggestion.

He studied his text more carefully, narrowing the points he hoped to make so the sermon resembled a rifle shot more than a shotgun blast. He concentrated on the words and delivery of his sermons more than ever. He discovered that this attention to content and delivery reduced redundancy. Through the additional work, the pastor became a better preacher. Because he reduced the length of his sermons, other problems were solved. Because the pastor heeded the suggestion of a member of the flock, the flock grew in their love and appreciation for him and for God and His Word.

The Bible directs us to "speak the truth" (Ephesians 4:25 NRSV). Although it doesn't say so directly, the Bible implies that Christians also should "hear the truth." Church workers are free in Christ to "check their egos" at the church door and concentrate on what's best for the congregation. Because we are assured that Christ fills our lives to overflowing with meaning and purpose, we can hear suggestions without feeling threatened. We can concentrate on the wisdom offered, respond accordingly, and even thank those who offered it. Such behavior shows a leadership that doesn't come from experience, but from God. Churches who are blessed by such Christ-centered leaders generally grow both numerically and spiritually.

May God grant us the grace to do more than just speak the truth. May we be the kind of disciples who hear the truth as well.

The Prayer: Heavenly Father, Your love in Christ declares that I am precious in Your sight. Strengthen me so I can hear the truth when others offer evaluations or suggestions. I ask this, Lord, so Your kingdom may grow. In Jesus' name. Amen.

~50~

Speaking the Truth in Love

> But speaking the truth in love, we must grow up in every way into Him who is the head, into Christ, from whom the whole body, joined and knit together by every ligament with which it is equipped, as each part is working properly, promotes the body's growth in building itself up in love. *Ephesians 4:15–16 (NRSV)*

"I was just being honest!" The words spewed from the husband's mouth as quickly as the tears streamed down his wife's cheeks. His words were cruel, but he took no responsibility for her pain. His vindication, he claimed, was that "he told it like it was"—the painful truth. He saw himself as virtuous, even as his helpmate sobbed.

Paul tells us the truth can hurt. A tenor may have a less than beautiful voice, but telling him the truth could break his heart. A Sunday school teacher may not have the gift of teaching, but flatly announcing this could change her relationships within the congregation forever. The maintenance person may be getting old, his job performance may be slipping, but being brutally frank may not solve the problem.

God knows the truth can hurt so He commands people not just to speak the truth, but to speak it in love. That's precisely how He deals with us. His Law condemns each of us. It reveals the truth that we are idolaters, blasphemers, absentee worshipers, disrespectful to those in authority, murderers, adulterers, thieves, gossips, and dissatisfied coveters. But this truth is always spoken in love—love hanging from the cross that separates our sin from us. With the proof of His love on His hands, feet, and side, Jesus shows us our sin, and we know He forgives it.

As Christians, when we witness the sin of others, we have a responsibility to say something, but we do it as one who has been forgiven. When the conversation ends, our brother or sister is no longer alone with the problem.

When God's people speak the truth in love, people grow in their effectiveness and witness for Jesus. When the sin-made-hypersensitive world sees that Christians can admonish one another peacefully and exhort one another, they seek the Savior who gives such power.

May God forbid that we ever declare in self-righteous glee, "I was just telling the truth." Instead, may we speak the truth in the love of Christ that has saved us from our sin.

The Prayer: Lord, I can become self-righteous when it comes to telling the truth. I sometimes think that because something is true, I am free to share it—even if it hurts or destroys another person. Help me to speak the truth in love so Your children may grow. In Your name. Amen.

~51~

Sinning on the Side of Omission

> But Thomas (who was called the Twin), one of the twelve, was not with them when Jesus came. So the other disciples told him, "We have seen the Lord." But he said to them, "Unless I see the mark of the nails in His hands, and put my finger in the mark of the nails and my hand in His side, I will not believe." *John 20:24–25 (NRSV)*

One type of sin is known as a sin of omission. Sins of omission are simple to commit. You just have to forget something you should do. Thomas committed a sin of omission when he failed to gather with Jesus' disciples in the Upper Room.

Not going to church, not remembering your parents' anniversary, and mistakenly planning your vacation during the week of VBS are just a few of the acts of omission for modern church workers.

We could make a long list of omissions that we have committed during our ministries. More important would be identifying the problems that give rise to these sins. In a word, it's self-centeredness. I easily can become so absorbed in how I feel about the voters' assembly rejecting my brilliant recommendation that I completely forget Mrs. Meyer's sister in my prayers. Church workers can become so upset because the congregation has "defiled" their sanctuary with "contemporary" worship forms that they forget about the choir member who had cataract surgery.

Sins of omission can powerfully effect a leader's ministry. When committed too often, they cause members to question how much the church worker cares for them. A church that has a defined sense of "family" is a church where sins of omission don't occur often. When they do, they are confessed immediately and reconciliation is begun. Churches who don't omit people, ideas, caring programs, and thank-yous are happy places in which to worship and serve.

One way to put aside the sins of omission is to remember these words from Ephesians: "For it is by grace you have been saved, through faith—and this is not from yourselves, it is the gift of God—not by works, so that no one can boast. For we are God's workmanship, created in Christ Jesus to do good works which God prepared in advance for us to do" (Ephesians 2:8–10).

People who transfer their focus from good works to God's grace take seriously God's proclamation that we are His workmanship, created to carry out His will. People who take seriously their Christ-secured position as God's workmanship remember birthdays and anniversaries. They remember the anniversaries of funerals and share words of support to those who grieve. They remember names so they can communicate personally in the name of Jesus.

On Judgment Day, when the Book of Life is opened and read, each of us will rejoice that God never commits an omission. Our names will be there. He will remember us. Thus Jesus asks us to offer gifts of "remembering" to all whom we serve.

The Prayer: God, You have such a phenomenal memory! You have remembered me in Your kingdom. Help me to remember the needs of others. In Your Holy name I pray. Amen.

～52～

Erring on the Side of Commission

> Then Moses summoned Bezalel and Oholiab and every skilled person to whom the LORD had given ability and who was willing to come and do the work. They received from Moses all the offerings the Israelites had brought to carry out the work of constructing the sanctuary. And the people continued to bring freewill offerings morning after morning. So all the skilled craftsmen who were doing all the work on the sanctuary left their work and said to Moses, "The people are bringing more than enough for doing the work the LORD commanded to be done." Then Moses gave an order and they sent this word throughout the camp: "No man or woman is to make anything else as an offering for the sanctuary." *Exodus 36:2–6*

Sins of commission happen when we do something that God doesn't want us to do. Often sins of commission offend not only God but also hurt others. That's the way we interpret it from a Christian perspective. The devil, however, would see sins of commission from a generously different angle. Satan would say we are "sinning" when we honor God. Indeed, from the devil's point of view, our works of service are "errors" on the side of commission.

God's people always have been good at "sinning"— against the devil, that is—on the side of commission. When it was time to build the tabernacle, Moses gathered gifts from the people. However, they contributed so much that Moses instructed them to stop giving. When Jacob was reunited with Esau, he tried to show his sincerity by sending thousands of cattle and sheep to capture his brother's heart. His brother didn't need the gifts, but Jacob wanted to make up for the earlier conflict. He "erred" on the side of commission, and God blessed it. People who find joy from being the disciples of Jesus, regularly "err" on matters of love, mercy, faith, and hope.

When our church's evangelism committee was asked whether they would hand out vacation Bible school pamphlets on both sides of the highway, they responded, "If we are going to err, let's err on the side of commission." They went to both sides. The VBS was a huge success.

Wouldn't it be wonderful if all our churches asked and answered questions about their ministry in the following way: Are we going to support a mission in Mexico or Moscow? "We'll do both." Are we going to add a preschool or a kindergarten to our church ministry? "Let's do both." Will we add a youth worker or a special education teacher to our staff? "We'll add both."

May God grant us such an experience of His power that none of us is afraid to put God to the challenge and stretch Him as much as He will allow. When it comes to erring, wouldn't we rather sin on the side of commission (in this context) than sin on the side of omission? Grant this Lord to us all.

The Prayer: Lord, You are able to accomplish in me far more than I could ever ask or think. Help me trust always in Your power that I may be generous in responding to Your love. In Jesus' name. Amen.

~53~

Maintaining Standards

Here is a trustworthy saying: If anyone sets his heart on being an overseer, he desires a noble task. Now the overseer must be above reproach, the husband of but one wife, temperate, self-controlled, respectable, hospitable, able to teach. *1 Timothy 3:1–2*

Perhaps you have been taught that "ambition" regarding church office is bad. We are to let the office seek the person. Today's words from St. Paul place that notion into question. St. Paul implies that "seeking an office" is acceptable, as long as those who seek the office meet certain criteria.

Although Paul's list of characteristics target overseers or "bishops," they are useful goals for all who are in church work. One who maintains the standards listed here will be free from scandal and gossip. It's not much fun to talk about someone who maintains a healthy marriage, doesn't blow up in angry episodes, doesn't have any "New Year's Eve" stories, and even loves her in-laws. Paul shares these words so we might declare with one voice, "Grant this, Lord, to us all!"

The truth is that such characteristics are sometimes not the possession of church workers past, present, or future. One of the most heartbreaking flaws is the one St. Paul lists first: "the husband of but one wife." Sexual improprieties have no place among those who proclaim that they will "adorn the Gospel of Christ with a holy life."

Yet we live in an imperfect world. Science and medicine tell us that people can possess strong sexual feelings. No one is exempt. It was in His goodness that God created male and female. It is in our sin that this arrangement became a problem. The ideal is that those who work together in the church will care for one another. We will go out of our way to assist one another. Such activity runs the risk of taking people to a line of inappropriateness, which, if crossed, drives workers into sin and the church into chaos.

Again Jesus gives us power and instruction to avoid such trouble. For example, Jesus makes it clear that we are to love the Lord our God with all our heart. If professional church workers develop inappropriate sexual feelings, the feelings can be stopped with God's help. The notion that we have feelings we can't control flies in the face of the Third Article of the Apostle's Creed. Daily the Holy Spirit calls, gathers, and enlightens His church. Enlightened Christian leaders ask God to keep them from behavior that is destructive to themselves and to the church.

Although the world readily accepts ethical relativity, that influence is counter to the thinking of those who serve the Lord. Regardless of how difficult a 25-year-old marriage has been, regardless of how cold a wife of 17 years has become, regardless of the fact that a man has lost the romance of earlier years, God never leads the disenchanted to adulterous relationships. It is never the will of God; it's just human will that becomes like a god.

To strengthen us against temptation, God has called us to care for one another. When people who work together enjoy trusting, honest, and forgiving relationships, they can confront one another in love regarding inappropriate behavior. Those confronted with their behavior can hear the words in love. Together they can ask forgiveness for Christ's sake and trust that God grants it, even as He will help repair the relationships and keep them healthy.

One danger inherent in human relationships is turning people into objects that supply our needs, physically or emotionally. Jesus equips us to treat people as precious and sacred to God. That's why St. Paul tells Timothy that he should treat all young women as sisters, with absolute purity. Let that be the Christ-given norm among all church workers—that we treat one another as brothers and sisters with all purity.

Sexual scandal abides everywhere in our world. Church workers who work together in honor and chastity lift high the cross of Christ. They abide by standards established by the Savior who died to forgive those who break the standards.

The Prayer: Dear Father, You know the history of Your church, including the sexual sins committed by its workers. I pray that I would not know such sin. Strengthen me in my love for You that I will turn aside from all temptation. Help me deal with my fellow workers and the people I serve as brothers and sisters. Also forgive those who have faltered. In Jesus' name. Amen.

~54~

Replace Yourself

"The harvest is plentiful, but the workers are few. Ask the Lord of the harvest, therefore, to send out workers into His harvest field." Luke 10:2

After I had addressed a group of high school kids, two young men approached me and said, "Pastor, you make working for the Lord sound as exciting as working for the CIA. Could we talk to you about being pastors?"

I was as astounded by their enthusiasm as they were with mine. As we talked, I learned that they thought church work was fraught with trouble and suffering. They were absolutely sure that church workers received more criticism in one year than they would like to face in their lifetimes. I told them that some of what they thought was true but that much of church work is wonderful and exciting.

I learned a lot that day about why churches have trouble recruiting workers. The work doesn't look like fun. This is a shame because it isn't true.

It is fun to open the sanctuary doors on Sunday morning and watch the pews fill with the faithful. It's fun to watch the child you baptized get confirmed and married. It is fun to watch children who left the church return, bringing little ones with them. It is fun to share meals with congregation members. It is fun to watch students grow up to support society and church as well-adjusted, faith-filled adults. Ministry is fun. We need to share that idea.

A smile is a great start. One church I served had a photograph of the pastor who had served there in the late 1800s. Each night I would leave the church and look at this man's scowling face. I wondered if his picture paralleled his personality. I asked his still-surviving children, and they affirmed that it was. "Everybody was afraid of him," his children said. I submit that church workers don't need to be feared. Respected? Honored? Yes! Feared? No!

One reason to remove fear is that it inspires few young people to enter church work. Kids are attracted to professions where people seem happy and satisfied. An even better reason to remove fear is that ministry properly demonstrates the joy of salvation earned by Jesus Christ.

On a practical level, church workers can strive to replace themselves. They can recruit at least one person to serve the Lord as a professional church worker. It's not hard to do. You don't need to bribe, cajole, or threaten kids. You just have to inspire them. You show them the joy in what you do so they want to live in that joy. It works.

I know pastors and teachers who are extraordinary at what they do. Others don't preach well or aren't exemplary teachers. Some disappoint people. Others come up with suggestions that no one appreciates. But they recruit church workers. They recruit them because kids see that they are happy in their profession.

We have much to do on a daily basis as church workers. We worry about the safety of our students, lesson plans, lunch money, and permission slips. There are Bible studies to prepare and funerals to conduct. Throughout the commotion and business, may God empower us to add one more thing: Inspire a young person to become a church worker.

The Prayer: Father, indeed the harvest is ripe and the workers are few. Thank You for calling me to be a worker in Your harvest. Make me a positive role model for others, especially for young people, a model that leads them joyfully into professional church work. In Jesus' name. Amen.

~55~

Thank You, God, That I Failed

And we know that in all things God works for the good of those who love Him, who have been called according to His purpose. *Romans 8:28*

If the devil is in the details, there are some of us who haven't seen Satan in years. I'm one of those people. Sometimes I feel intimidated by church workers who know all the details.

I once found myself serving at a special celebration service with a man who has a reputation for details. He prepared the service and served as officiant. I was the preacher. We had been blessed by the Word through the beautiful service he wrote. In the middle of the Lord's Supper, he suddenly looked at me with such panic on his face that I thought we were having an earthquake. He whispered, "We are out of wine." His whisper quickly turned into an announcement, "We're out of communion wine."

After the service, the worshipers responded as though nothing had happened. They were enjoying fellowship and were congratulating and thanking the large choir. I looked for my friend. He had moved behind a curtain with his head down. He felt he had sinned because he had forgotten a detail. "There are lots of people who forget details every day and question their usefulness as church workers because of it," I said. "You are an obviously useful church worker. You forgot a detail, but you still served many people today. Rejoice, my friend, God is using you."

That's the way it is for church workers when we fail. Failures may be disasters to us, but to the people we serve, they are powerful reminders that God works through His Word despite human weaknesses. When we know that God uses even our failures, we don't need to fear failure. If God takes care of the big details like justification and sanctification, He can also handle the little details of our ministries.

An oft-quoted phrase attributed to Martin Luther is "Sin boldly, but believe more boldly still." Luther wanted us to know that in this broken world, all our actions contain some remnant of evil. None of our motives or actions are pure. Therefore, Luther implies that instead of becoming obsessive about failures, we should act and serve, fully trusting that Jesus' death and resurrection have unleashed a power that covers our failures.

The Prayer: Lord, I am justified by grace through faith in Christ Jesus. Because of Him, You have wrapped me in Your love and You can use my failures for the good of the Church. Help me rest and work in that confidence today and every day. In Jesus' name. Amen.

I Failed

Then seizing Him, they led Him away and took Him into the house of the high priest. Peter followed at a distance. But when they had kindled a fire in the middle of the courtyard and had sat down together, Peter sat down with them. A servant girl saw him seated there in the firelight. She looked closely at him and said, "This man was with Him." But he denied it. "Woman, I don't know Him," he said. A little later someone else saw him and said, "You also are one of them." "Man, I am not!" Peter replied. About an hour later another asserted, "Certainly this fellow was with Him, for he is a Galilean." Peter replied, "Man, I don't know what you're talking about!" Just as he was speaking, the rooster crowed. The Lord turned and looked straight at Peter. Then Peter remembered the word the Lord had spoken to him: "Before the rooster crows today, you will disown Me three times." And he went outside and wept bitterly. *Luke 22:54–62*

Peter failed. He had an opportunity to support the Son of God, but he failed several times. He failed when he slept in the Garden of Gethsemane. He failed when he cut off Malchus' ear, and he failed when he denied knowing Jesus. If Peter had worked for a Fortune 500 company, he would have been fired.

Peter didn't work for a Fortune 500 company. He worked for God. Accomplishment and performance are different in the kingdom of God than they are the kingdom of humans. In the human kingdom, Peter would be remembered as a dismal failure, deserving termination. He would be punished so no one else would perform so poorly.

The gospels record Peter's actions, but not in a way that brings terror into the hearts of others. He is lifted up as a failure whom God changed and strengthened so he could continue to serve. That's what God does with people who fail. He loves, motivates, changes, and makes them models who demonstrate His strength even in their own weakness.

I thank God for Peter's failure. It reminds me that I'm no different than any of those whom Jesus made servants in the kingdom. Jesus can do the same for me. He can even do the same for others through my failures.

That's God's promise for every church worker. He doesn't just bless our successes, He brings good from our failures. He blesses our failures in two ways.

First, He blesses the outcome of our failures. I once "failed" when the elders of our congregation instructed me to visit a young woman who was pregnant and unmarried. The girl chose to have the baby and live in her mother's home—a home that already had four people living in it. The elders and the mother of the girl were sure that the baby would hurt everyone involved, including the baby. I spoke with the mother, but I failed. She would not give up her baby for adoption. I left the meeting feeling like a failure. After the baby was born, I heard how terrible life was in that home. With every report, I felt worse. While I was feeling bad about my failure, God was at work to make it a blessing. He brought my younger brother into the life of this young mother. They met, fell in love, and married. The boy whom I hoped would be given up for adoption is now my nephew! He is an incredible blessing to our family.

Thank God that I failed. Or was it really a failure?

Second, people who see us fail are blessed. The failures of church leaders allow members of the church to accept their own failures, ask forgiveness, and move on. There is nothing wrong when church members say to themselves or, for that matter, to others, "Well, my pastor or teacher messed up. I guess it's all right that I messed up too. God has forgiven me, and He will help me do better next time."

I always try to get things right in my ministry, but truthfully, I've given up worrying about it. It's not that I don't care about doing my best. I've just learned how God blesses others despite my failures. I'm not afraid of my failures anymore.

The Prayer: God, thank You for turning my failures into blessings. Keep me from allowing Your goodness to make me lazy or complacent. Instead, help me to live thankfully and in the confidence that You will make me more than I could ever ask or think. In Jesus' name. Amen.

~57~

The Pursuit of Excellence

> But speaking the truth in love, we must grow up in every way into Him who is the head, into Christ, from whom the whole body, joined and knit together by every ligament with which it is equipped, as each part is working properly, promotes the body's growth in building itself up in love. *Ephesians 4:15–16 (NRSV)*

A pastor friend of mine once joked that he hadn't read a book in 10 years and that no books on his office bookshelf were published after 1950. In other words, he had done little to improve himself since graduation. No, God's Word hasn't changed since 1950, but certainly a seminary education does not by itself prepare anyone for a lifetime of ministry.

The same problem plagues teachers. Just because we got a degree in education in 1955, it doesn't mean we are equipped to teach children until the year 2000. Teachers, pastors, deaconesses, and DCEs need to do what Paul tells the church at Ephesus: "Grow up in every way into Him who is the head, into Christ."

Who would allow a physician who hadn't learned the latest techniques in heart surgery to perform a coronary bypass? Is it any different for people who bring the saving news of Christ into the homes of students and members?

An emphasis on growing new skills is nothing new for church workers. During His ministry, Jesus continually helped His disciples grow in faith and skill. He couldn't let them go through their ministries shouting down people who were casting out demons in His name. He told them, "He who is not against us is for us." He repeatedly taught them that the Gentiles are also welcome in the kingdom of God so they would be courageous proclaimers of this divine salvation plan equally to all.

Jesus comes among us as well and encourages us to keep growing in our skills. To take classes, attend lectures, and enroll in seminars is to let the people we serve know that we care about them and our Christ-called service to them.

Once my neighbor and I attended a debate between physicians and members of the clergy. The physicians shared their discoveries about in vitro fertilization, cloning, and other discoveries that affect the birth process. My neighbor has never had a high regard for the clergy, but he was astounded that professional church workers could know so much about the issue. He couldn't believe that they would take time to become aware of scientific research. When the debate ended, he had a renewed respect for the church.

For whatever reason, many people truly believe that church workers are not as aware as those who work in other professions. This has never been acceptable to Jesus, who declared that we should love the Lord our God with all our heart, all our soul, and all our minds. He wants our profession to be honored by the world so we represent Him with integrity, intelligence, and care.

No matter what kind of church work we do, a requirement of excellence doesn't come only from a principal or senior pastor. It comes from God—a God who hopes that no group of teachers would ever do what one group did years ago at a conference.

The speaker was powerful and practical, but I saw many teachers correcting papers. First, I considered this rude. The man had come miles to help us in our ministry. Second, they were missing information vital to the growth of our ministry. I talked with individual teachers privately and encouraged them to participate in the lecture. They refused. I became so upset, I left. As the years went by, I learned that teachers who had the greatest trouble with parents and students were those who turned deaf ears to those who wanted to help them develop their skills.

May God lay on our hearts both the opportunity and the blessing to grow in our skills, to be better practitioners of our art than we were the year before. Jesus will provide us with the opportunity. We can trust that every new thing we learn may some day and in some way be used by God.

The Prayer: Lord Jesus, You know me. Sometimes I allow myself to be puffed up with pride over my skills and learning. Remind me that You continually bless me with new learning so I can better serve You and Your people. Take from me all pride, O Lord, and make me Your ever-growing servant. In Your name. Amen.

~58 ~

Our Families and Those Who Watch Them

A bishop then must be blameless, the husband of one wife, temperate, sober-minded, of good behavior, hospitable, able to teach; not given to wine, not violent, not greedy for money, but gentle, not quarrelsome, not covetous; one who rules his own house well, having his children in submission with all reverence (for if a man does not know how to rule his own house, how will he take care of the church of God?). *1 Timothy 3:2–5 (NKJV)*

It didn't take long for the news to hit our congregation's information superhighway. My daughter, Rebecca, in the heat of an eighth-grade volleyball game, had fussed at a referee. Her classmates immediately converged on her and said, "Becca, you can't talk like that. You are the preacher's daughter!" In utter frustration, she stood in the center of the court and hollered, "I am not the preacher's daughter! I am Rebecca Rogers!"

Over the years, I have watched hundreds of volleyball games. In each one, I'm sure someone lost their temper. They may have said something we've taught Christian children they shouldn't say. But no one ever felt like they needed to report the activity to me. When my daughter showed her humanity, several people felt "led" to tell me she had an out-burst on the court. It was hard for me not to get angry at their heightened sense of righteousness when it came to my child.

Here is how I responded: "You know, one thing that my children didn't count on when they were born is that their father would live in the fishbowl and take his family members with him. My daughter is young and still believes that she's free to be herself and free to count on forgiveness. I guess it'll take her a while to learn that people are more anxious to judge her than to forgive her. I'm sure some of you folks will help her learn her lesson soon."

Thankfully, not one of those "well-intentioned folks" had much to say in response. I hope they took the time to think about how difficult it is for the professional church worker's family when people don't offer them the same grace as they expect to be shown to them.

We who live in the kingdom's fishbowl need to know how to survive the scrutiny of those we serve. First, it is our business to proclaim the forgiveness of sins in Word and deed to everyone we serve, even those who criticize our family. We proclaim and live this forgiveness as though the well-being of our family depends on it. When we forgive as Jesus forgives us, we establish a climate of forgiveness, and others will grow in mercy and grace.

Second, it's vitally important that church workers communicate to their families the precarious and some-times unfair role they play. Our families need to know that here, too, we forgive the sinner and ask God for the strength to rise above it all. Certainly Jesus will answer that prayer and give us strength because He Himself was held to human expectations. He loved His way through such criti-cism, and He strengthens us to do the same.

As a child, I walked with a large and noticeable limp. I was, of course, a target for all the less-than-sensitive kids in school. I would come home with a bruised ego and cry. My mother would instruct me to pray that my antagonists might grow up and see the beauty of God in every creation. Mom turned the tables. Instead of making me think I had to stand there and take it, she taught me that God would use me to teach and help others. She taught me to follow the gracious and merciful example of Jesus.

My dear brothers and sisters in church work, it's still the truth. When you and yours receive criticism, pray and lead them into a Christ-centered, effective life.

The Prayer: Lord Jesus, again I thank You for calling me into the harvest field. I ask You to help loved ones in the face of criticism. When that criticism comes, help us to love and forgive those who judge us. In Your name. Amen.

~59~

Patience in Ministry

Then He told this parable: "A man had a fig tree planted in his vineyard; and he came looking for fruit on it
and found none. So he said to the gardener, 'See here!
For three years I have come looking for fruit on this fig
tree, and still I find none. Cut it down! Why should it
be wasting the soil?' He replied, 'Sir, let it alone for one
more year, until I dig around it and put manure on it.
If it bears fruit next year, well and good; but if not, you
can cut it down.' " *Luke 13:6–9 (NRSV)*

I once had avocado trees. I always had wanted to own
one. My father had an avocado tree—a big one. It bore hundreds of avocados each year. I enjoyed those avocados. We
had them for lunch and dinner. In California, where I grew
up, it was perfectly acceptable for poor kids to have avocado
sandwiches for school. I know because I did. Because of all of
this, I love avocados.

I love avocados so much that I try to raise avocado
trees. Frankly, it's not going well. I've lost one tree already.
My other tree looks as though it will die too. I'm patient with
it. I cultivate around it. I give it plenty of water. I talk to the
leaves. I've promised to buy it another avocado tree so it can
have company.

My friends laugh and tease me for all the care I take
with this avocado tree—a tree that has blessed me with only
three avocados in seven years! But I tell them the bottom line
for me is that I love avocados. I will do whatever it takes to
make them grow. Right now, I have no physical reason to

believe that I will have much of an avocado harvest anytime soon. But I believe the day will come.

I share this with you because it seems that's the way it goes with people in ministry. We ask others to get involved in the Lord's work, but those who do are fewer than we would like. We encourage many to change their lifestyles, but those who follow our suggestions are few indeed. We may get upset over this. It is easy to become frustrated and claim that we don't have time for people who don't cooperate with our suggestions. Our sinful nature calls us to part company with the counselee who won't take our suggestions seriously. When we work with families who need to make wholesale changes yet continue to offer excuses why this can't happen, we are tempted to wash our hands of them.

Jesus is the master of patience. He seems to work on a schedule that none of us knows about. It is a schedule that comes from the most high God. And thank God He uses it! If His time frame were the same as ours, Israel would have been in trouble. David, Paul, and Peter would have been cut off from the grace of God. God continues to work with the same timing He used when He sent Jesus to save the world—just the right time.

So it goes for us. We who have received patience from God avoid hastily deciding that some children don't belong in our school. We avoid precipitous decisions about who should and who should not serve in our churches. Instead we wait.

We aren't waiting on a person to figure out his or her personality flaws and become someone new. Instead, we are waiting to see how God can use people who are less than perfect to do His will. When we wait on Jesus, we see things happen. It took Peter time to become a champion of the faith, but, by God's grace, it happened. It took time for Paul to become a champion of the faith, but, by God's grace, it happened. It will take time for each of us to become a champion of the faith, but the Holy Spirit will work in us through the Word too. It will take time for the people we serve to become champions of the faith, but in His own time, Jesus will do it.

God, through His Word, encourages us to be slow in judgment as we evaluate the progress of others. God doesn't want us to get in His way. Instead, we watch and see what good things come to the people and the church workers who are patient.

The Prayer: Dear Lord Jesus, You know I cannot be perfect. As a church worker, sometimes I have little patience with my coworkers and the people I serve. Help me to be patient that I might ultimately see what God has in store for these dear people. In Your name. Amen.

Money and Ministry

> But she said, "As the LORD your God lives, I have nothing baked, only a handful of meal in a jar, and a little oil in a jug; I am now gathering a couple of sticks, so that I may go home and prepare it for myself and my son, that we may eat it, and die." Elijah said to her, "Do not be afraid; go and do as you have said; but first make me a little cake of it and bring it to me, and afterwards make something for yourself and your son. For thus says the LORD the God of Israel: The jar of meal will not be emptied and the jug of oil will not fail until the day that the LORD sends rain on the earth." *1 Kings 17:12–14 (NRSV)*

Our oldest daughter did well in high school. She earned good grades and performed well enough athletically for acceptance into some of the finest universities. Her significant liability was that her father and mother were both church workers. She also has two sisters and a brother who also want to attend college. She had prepared a list of the schools she wanted to attend. Although we did our best to prepare financially for her education, we couldn't afford to send her to her first choice.

The sorrow that invaded our home covered us with gloom. Although our daughter did her best to maintain a positive appearance, her mother and I could tell that her heart was broken. I decided to take my feelings out on God directly. My prayers were anything but reverent. The word *why* showed up again and again. "How could You?" was another frequent phrase in my prayers. I felt as though God had let us down in our ability to care for our children.

I hate to admit it, but I even began to resent the people we serve. Although we serve people who have enough money to send their children to the schools of their choice, those same people don't compensate church workers so they might enjoy the same blessing. That hurt a lot.

Then the strangest thing happened. A letter bearing the seal of the great state of California was delivered to our home. Our daughter took the letter from the mailbox and asked me what I thought it contained. Feeling pretty cynical, I said, "It's probably a bill. When do we get anything from the government that isn't a bill?"

She opened the letter. "Dad, it says here that the State of California is granting me the money I need to attend the school of my choice," she said. A grant! I couldn't believe it. I was so skeptical that I called the state to verify this document. The unbelievable was true! The grant was awarded on the basis of need and merit. I hugged my daughter. "We both did our jobs," I said. "You took care of the merit, and I took care of the need!" We both laughed. It felt good to laugh again.

The next person I spoke to was God. It was time to apologize for being surly. I had no historical rationale for being so upset. God always has provided for our family. We have everything we need to live comfortably in the promise that God will "give us this day our daily bread." He always has. He always will. Even more important, God took care of our biggest need—the need to be saved from sin.

Don't lose sight of that truth when it looks as though God has "short-changed" us. Elijah and the widow help us keep our focus. They weren't looking for smoked salmon, filet mignon, or fine wine. They were satisfied with flour and oil. Instead of complaining about what they didn't have, they saw God's powerful hand in the flour and oil. They knew God would give them what they needed.

Each of us has a similar story. When we share stories of how God provides for us, it's not the same as bragging. It's more like a celebration because what God does for one, He will do for all. We can tell our stories of "deliverance" to those we serve. Our stories may help them to put their lives in perspective also. It encourages them to develop Christ-centered priorities and values.

The Prayer: Almighty God, You open Your hand and satisfy the desires of every living thing. May Your grace fill me with such confidence that I am always satisfied with what You give. May my life serve as a model for others. In Jesus' name. Amen.

~ 61 ~

Enjoy the Applause

Therefore, since we are surrounded by so great a cloud of witnesses, let us also lay aside every weight and the sin that clings so closely, and let us run with perseverance the race that is set before us. *Hebrews 12:1 (NRSV)*

Personally, I've never experienced thousands upon thousands of people cheering for me, but I love to watch sports-related movies. Almost always they are stories of "crucifixion and resurrection." A promising athlete with nothing but a positive future is struck by some adversity and must work hard to attain success. Powerful music accompanies the scenes to bring the audience to an emotional high. An absolutely necessary part of these scenes is applause. The applause lubricates the entire proceeding. Once the victory is won, the applause turns into unbridled celebration. I always walk away from those movies ready to take on the world.

It doesn't take long for me to realize that this was just a movie. Often, people don't support or cheer those who have challenges. In our sinful world, there are too few encouragers, people who applaud us on to victory.

My grandfather was a tremendous encourager. Gramps would come to watch me play Little League baseball and cheer me on, even during games when our team had no hope of winning. After the game, he would point out something I had done well. Knowing that he paid such close attention filled me with joy and a sense of importance.

I miss my grandfather, but reading Hebrews 12:1 after his death, I'm sure that not much has changed. This verse declares that we are surrounded by a great cloud of witnesses, that is, we are surrounded by the saints of God who cheer our work for the kingdom. I think that means that our grandfathers, grandmothers, fathers, mothers, husbands, wives, children—all who have gone on before us—are aware of the ways the Holy Spirit works through us. We are encouraged by knowing that. We might even hear the applause.

The applause is rightly for the star of our team, Jesus Christ. He truly deserves all the credit for winning the biggest of all contests. Yet He shares His glory as He enables us to serve Him through the Word. He has placed us on His team and will make us part of the "cloud of witnesses."

The challenge that God places before us is the ability to hear the applause. Daily, church workers encounter difficulties that could muffle the applause for Jesus and His team. Churches who have financial difficulties can create a cacophony that drowns out the joyful victory of salvation. Church workers who have trouble at home may be deaf to Jesus' encouragement.

But the applause remains. The saints are cheering, and they will never stop, even when we make mistakes. They won't stop cheering when we find ourselves confused or disoriented. They don't stop cheering because they know how it all turns out. You see, despite our troubles and weakness, we do triumph, we do win. Jesus covers us with His power and grace and gives us the victory. The cheers are for

Him. Because the cheers are for Him, they are also for us.

I believe that if joy came just from the results of my ministry, I would be depressed most of the time. But our joy comes from other places. Our joy comes from knowing that God blesses ministry in ways we may never understand. The "cloud of witnesses" understands that and celebrates! When we remain focused on our task, lifting high the cross at every opportunity, then our "witnesses" rejoice, as does our Father in heaven.

May Jesus enable us all to hear the applause of the witnesses for His victory. May their applause and that of our Father in heaven encourage us until that day when we join the cloud of witnesses.

The Prayer: Heavenly Father, thank You for the great cloud of witnesses that surround me. They are evidence of Your saving love and grace. Help me to be so strengthened so I may stay faithful in my ministry, even in times of stress and trial. In Jesus' name. Amen.

~62~

The Simple Life of Prayer

Rejoice always, pray without ceasing, give thanks in all circumstances; for this is the will of God in Christ Jesus for you. *1 Thessalonians 5:16–18 (NRSV)*

I've heard some beautiful prayers. Many pastors can stand before the altar and offer prayers suitable for publication. My Sunday school teachers could put the desires of their hearts into amazing words. When I was confirmed, my congregation gave me a copy of a prayer book. I still use it. The prayers in it are masterpieces of praise and prose.

Because I was surrounded by such masterful pray-ers, I found it difficult to understand St. Paul's direction that we should "Rejoice always, pray without ceasing." Prayer words never came easily to me. I would get confused about whether I should refer to the most high God as "Thee" or just "You." Every night I tried to offer prayers worthy of God's attention. I even remember falling asleep in mid-prayer because I couldn't think of the perfect way to express my need. "Pray without ceasing" didn't seem like a blessing to me; instead, it seemed an incredible burden that I couldn't bear.

Then I became a father. A father's job is to provide for the needs of his children. In that way, an earthly father might be compared to God: He wants to meet his children's needs. From the very first, the "petitions" of my children were not literary masterpieces. They were screams. I puzzled long and hard, wondering if my children wanted to be changed, fed, rocked, or, as our pediatrician said, they were "just getting some exercise." Because I didn't know for sure what they needed, I gave them everything I could.

As my children grew older, their ability to communicate improved, but it still wasn't perfect. I remember one Sunday afternoon, my son was having lunch. He was 2, sitting smartly in his high chair. He was enjoying his Sabbathday repast when suddenly he lifted high his little plastic cup and pointed it toward me. He used no words, but I could tell what he wanted—milk. I quickly poured some milk. He smiled and said "tatu." It was then that I began to understand what St. Paul meant when he told us to "Rejoice always, pray without ceasing."

My children never used sophisticated words to speak when they wanted something. They didn't have to because I was their dad. I figured out what they needed. Sometimes I even provided for them without a single verbal request on their part. I could do that because I loved them. I was focused on their needs. Therefore, my children didn't need to say, "Father, thou from whose loins I came, thou who hast provided me with food for the body and shelter from the storm, I beseech you this night that you might open the rectangular appliance filled with Freon and provide me with a generous helping of the fruit of the cow." "Dad, can I have some milk?" was fine.

God is our Father. As a good Father, He responds to simple prayers. God hears and responds when we simply ask on the way to work that we would be a blessing to our students. A simple, "O God, no!" offered when a child falls headfirst onto the concrete playground is good enough. Silent prayers of no more than "Help us, God" when we're involved in a difficult congregational meeting are acceptable. You see, it's not the prayers that motivate or awaken God. It's God's love that brings Him to our aid.

If the utterances that come spontaneously and reflect the needs of our souls are prayers, then it becomes easy to see how we can pray without ceasing. The key to prayer without ceasing is not the propriety of inspired words. It's simply the knowledge that God is listening to us.

In addition to looking at prayer books, we also can speak from our hearts the words, phrases, grunts, and groans that express our condition. Our Father who loves us, who understands our every action, will deliver us.

God wants us to know that at times when we are so distraught that we can't utter our own prayer, the Holy Spirit prays for us in God's language. Yes, God invites us to pray without ceasing, and He so wonderfully inclines His ear that He makes sure we do pray without ceasing.

The Prayer: Dearest Father, thank You for hearing my prayers, regardless of how they are phrased. Thank You that when I am unable to pray, Your Spirit prays for me. In Jesus' name. Amen.

~ 63 ~

God and His People Keep Their Word

"But I say to you, Do not swear at all, either by heaven, for it is the throne of God, or by the earth, for it is His footstool, or by Jerusalem, for it is the city of the great King. And do not swear by your head, for you cannot make one hair white or black. Let your word be 'Yes, Yes' or 'No, No'; anything more than this comes from the evil one." *Matthew 5:34–37 (NRSV)*

Many years ago, a principal got into a dispute with the chairman of the board of his school. The dispute developed from the principal's need to demonstrate that he had the school under control and didn't need assistance from the board. Contributing to this was the board president's need to keep the principal in his place.

The two men took to doing things on their own without the permission or knowledge of the other. When what had been done would come to the attention of the whole board, an argument between these two would ensue. Each one accused the other of being less than truthful. Each offered excuses for doing things without the board's permission. Chaos reigned, and the school suffered. I remember asking a teacher how things were going. Her reply stunned me. "Nobody around here speaks the truth, so how could anyone know how things are going?"

Jesus tells us that conduct for church workers includes telling the truth. Jesus said it clearly. Let your "yes" be "yes" and your "no" be "no." In other words, mean what you say and make sure what you say is the truth. Any other embellishment, explanation, excuse, or complaint tends to erode people's confidence.

A church worker once came to me nearly hysterical. He told me that something horrible had happened regarding the registration for a national youth gathering. Supposedly, the national office made a mistake and we would have to stay in a more expensive hotel—$7,000 more expensive! I believed everything he said and appealed to the congregation for the money. The people responded generously, and the money was raised within three weeks.

One morning while speaking with our business manager, I commented that our youth worker looked a whole lot better now that we had raised the money to cover the national office's mistake. The business manager gave me a cynical look. "That's what he told you?" he asked. "That's a long way away from the truth. The man didn't do what he was supposed to do when he was supposed to do it. It's a miracle they are getting in. He just didn't want you to know the truth."

I confronted the church worker. He turned red and walked away. He didn't stay in ministry much longer. A breach of trust is hard to deal with for both the offender and the offended. Jesus covered us with a magnificent amount of love and grace to overcome these difficulties.

People make mistakes all the time, and the church's business is the forgiveness of sins. Jesus freed us from guilt and shame so we can say "I'm sorry. I've done wrong. Please forgive me. Let's see if we can't make this better together."

I had a strong feeling about three school families who

had been less than helpful during their years at our school. They complained constantly and shared their discontent with anyone who would listen. The last straw came when they moved their children to another school, owing us $6,000 in tuition. I directed our business manager to take the steps necessary, even small claims court, to recover the loss. We outlined our options and I assumed he was proceeding with a solution. Six months later, I asked him the outcome of the tuition problem. The business manger looked at me and said, "Pastor, we've made no headway at all, and let me tell you why. I think it is the wrong thing to do. I wish you had dropped the whole thing."

His words flew over me like a breath of fresh air. I didn't appreciate what he had done, but I certainly appreciated his truthfulness. I shared my disappointment and encouraged him to share his feelings and thoughts with me immediately, especially when he disagreed with me. Two Christians let their "yes" be "yes" and their "no" be "no," and God caused respect and appreciation to grow between them.

Our world has degenerated to the point where it accepts lying as a part of life. Children can lie to their parents and receive no real consequence. Spouses can lie to each other and pray that they don't get caught. Elected officials can lie and their constituents laugh about it. This results in a total erosion of honor and trust. When "yes" doesn't mean "yes," and "no" doesn't mean "no," then no one is safe.

God lifts up His church workers to demonstrate the free and healthy lives that come to people who tell the truth. God wants us to show the world a community of people who believe that it is more important to tell the truth than it is to avoid the natural consequence of mistakes. Just as I grew closer to the business manager, so people will become closer to us and to our Lord as we respond truthfully. Imagine how a whole community of faith can grow when people who promise to pray for one another keep that promise. Consider the unity in a community where people who volunteer for tasks keep their word and show up.

Yes and *no* are small words, but when we use them in the power of Christ, they become a strong foundation on which to build a healthy church and community.

The Prayer: Heavenly Father, by the power of Your Spirit working through the Word, make my words truthful and honorable. I long to earn the trust, honor, and respect of those I serve. O Lord, open my lips so my "yes" is "yes" and my "no" is "no." In Jesus' name. Amen.

~ 64 ~

Suffer the Children

People were bringing little children to Jesus to have Him touch them, but the disciples rebuked them. When Jesus saw this, He was indignant. He said to them, "Let the little children come to Me, and do not hinder them, for the kingdom of God belongs to such as these." *Mark 10:13–14*

Olivia has been coming to church since she was three weeks old. Because the church doesn't provide child care at the Saturday night service, Olivia always stayed with her parents and two older brothers. Olivia is in no way a mean, disruptive child, but as she grew, she would walk up and down the pews during the service. She would sing whenever she wanted—sometimes even when the congregation sang. Although no one complained to her parents, I'm sure some believed that Olivia got nothing from the service. I'm sure others thought that worship would be less disrupted if Olivia stayed home.

Last Rally Day, Olivia, as a 3-year-old, became an official part of our Sunday school. As part of this recognition, she received her own offering envelopes. Her mother and father instructed her that this is where she places her gifts for Jesus. Olivia was thrilled to have such a "grown-up" thing as offering envelopes.

Olivia's parents take the stewardship training of their children seriously. Each of their children has three jars. They put their weekly tithe in one. In another, they save money. In the third jar, they place money to spend.

One Sunday afternoon, Olivia's mother heard sobbing from Olivia's room. She ran inside and saw Olivia sitting in a sea of offering envelopes, trying to return them to their box. You see, when Olivia came home from Rally Day, she took out all three jars and began to place "one moneys" into each envelope so she wouldn't miss a single week. Not being able to put the full envelopes back into the box frustrated the poor child.

Her mother, astounded at her daughter's joyful stewardship, helped her return each envelope to the box. She reminded Olivia that to fill all her envelopes, she had completely emptied all three jars. She had no more money. Olivia told her mother that she knew that, but "the most important thing was that none of Jesus' children go without a gift."

As her mother shared this story, I thought about those Saturday nights that Olivia wasn't "getting anything out of worship" and perhaps distracting other worshipers. I know better now. Jesus was at work in this child every time she heard the Word, whether she heard it while drawing on a visitor card or while dancing on the pew. She heard it, and the fruit of the Spirit is obvious.

Olivia stands before us as an example of what God accomplishes in His children. We can be advocates and allies of God's children. Reexamine today's trend of removing children from worship because they "don't get anything out of it" in the light of our understanding of Baptism. If God can give the gift of faith through water and the Word to an infant, how can we question what God can accomplish in children who attend worship?

Chances are good Jesus wasn't much appreciated when He gathered children to Himself. The time He spent with children took away from the time He spent with "real people." But Jesus disregarded the opinions of those who didn't see what He was accomplishing in those children. It's the same for us. God has given these children advocates to keep them within earshot of His Word, and we are those advocates. May God help us to provide opportunities for all the Olivias.

The Prayer: Lord, adult Christians sometimes take themselves too seriously. I sometimes become upset when Your dear children get in the way of the time I spend with You. Jesus, help me always to gather the children around You in church and Sunday school. In Your name. Amen.

~65~

I Hear You, Lord

Then one of the seraphs flew to me, holding a live coal that had been taken from the altar with a pair of tongs. The seraph touched my mouth with it and said: "Now that this has touched your lips, your guilt has departed and your sin is blotted out." Then I heard the voice of the Lord saying, "Whom shall I send, and who will go for Us?" And I said, "Here am I; send me!" *Isaiah 6:6–8 (NRSV)*

I worry about the call. Not that God won't take care of the manner by which He calls pastors into service. I'm afraid that we are becoming less capable of hearing His voice when He calls. For example, some congregations think that a church worker is neither a public minister nor a servant but is more like a hired hand. Being hired hands, if pastors do what their congregations expect, they are successful. If they call the congregation slow to account for some unfaithfulness or misdeed, they are removed.

During my ministry, I have witnessed a move from trusting the Holy Spirit to bring the right church workers into congregations to watching congregations arrange interviews and screen candidates. All this happens while the individual has a call to serve in the present ministry. It seems to me that such activity can be a blatant and selfish disregard for what God has established in another congregation.

I am not completely convinced that the "fault" for this approach to securing church workers lies with congregations. I'm afraid the fault sometimes lies with church workers.

Church workers are placed by God into service where He wants them to be. They serve enthusiastically because they know God sent them there. I think some church workers have lost this passionate commitment to the call. When that happens, workers look for more than an opportunity to serve. They begin looking for a location that meets their needs, a salary that will raise their lifestyle, a theological approach to ministry that matches their own understanding of theology and practice. The tragedy is that people move away from a trust in God and encourage a trust in self.

I believe that many difficulties that surround the call are resolved when church workers pray to hear the unimpeded voice of the Holy Spirit. The New Testament shows that Peter, Paul, Barnabas, and Silas never allowed their own situations to govern where they would go to preach the Gospel nor did it determine for them how long they would stay. Their sights were set not on owning a home or on retirement. Their sights were clearly set on Jesus.

For the sake of the church and its workers, we need to see our calling as different from hiring opportunities that secular businesses provide. We are servants of the most high God. He calls people into ministry today as He did Peter, Paul, James, and John.

One way to demonstrate that ministry differs from other jobs is for church workers to recognize when their ministries are coming to an end. When church workers realize that they have little more to offer through their specific skills and gifts, it may be time to serve where God can use those talents more. When a church worker no longer finds joy in ministry, perhaps it's time to ask God for some other work outside the public ministry. As church workers, we ask God to keep the ears of His servants open to His leading and to make His voice louder than the voice of selfishness.

May God rid His church and His church workers of the secular side of their personalities so the church might simply hear the Word of Christ and humbly follow where He leads.

The Prayer: Lord Jesus, You call people into many areas of service. Help me focus my ears completely on Your voice and not the voices of the world. May I trust You to place me where You would have me. In Your name. Amen.

~66~

Monument Makers

As you come to Him, the living Stone—rejected by men but chosen by God and precious to Him—you also, like living stones, are being built into a spiritual house to be a holy priesthood, offering spiritual sacrifices acceptable to God through Jesus Christ. *1 Peter 2:4–5*

Monuments are impressive. They generally stand tall, calling attention to themselves and to the issues they want us to remember. Those who build monuments have an intimate encounter with the person or event they are trying to honor. This intimate encounter often changes their lives. In the same way, those who visit monuments, such as the Washington Monument or the Vietnam War Memorial, often leave those places changed forever.

God would have us see that each church, school, or agency we serve stands tall as a monument to God's love in Christ. Each monument has some architectural uniqueness that sets it apart from other structures. The churches we serve are likewise to be set apart from other structures. The difference, however, is that the uniqueness of the church isn't architectural, it is internal. Peter gives us insight into how differences can be shown to the world. It's done through sacrifice. I believe it is fair to say that congregations follow the example of their leadership. As people see us sacrificing our time, talent, and treasure, they are inspired to greater acts of sacrifice themselves.

What this means is that while we work hard to make our church a splendid monument to the love of Christ, God is at work making us monuments to His love in Christ.

There was a time when the children of this country had many heroes. Athletes, public servants, Scout leaders, coaches, and the like provided youngsters with role models. Today, our children's heroes often seem bent on violence and destruction. Instead of providing leadership in the community, modern "heroes" demand more and more money for their services, behave as though they are above the law, and sometimes even take their own lives. These people serve as monuments to the presence and practices of Satan!

The exciting thing for church workers is that God is at work, making us monuments to His grace and mercy. We don't need to hit home runs or play a blaring guitar. When we give time to a young person or to a family member, God lifts us up as a monument to Christ's love. Each time we do good for others, God lifts us up as a monument to the Savior's care. Every hand we hold or shoulder we offer, every late-night phone call we receive without resentment allows God to mold us into models of compassion and decency. God makes us His monuments as we strive to make His church a monument. God makes us monuments to salvation, which will change and inspire lives forever. This spiritual monument will outlast human monuments. This monument will last through eternity.

Some of you reading this book have served me and the members of my family in a monumental way. This provides me with the opportunity to give thanks to God for you— monumental thanks!

The Prayer: Lord, move powerfully among Your church workers so congregations stand tall as monuments to Your love in Christ. At the same time, make us sacrificing servants so we, too, might be monuments dedicated to You in this world. In Your precious and powerful name. Amen.

~ 67 ~

Putting the Best Construction on Everyone

Perhaps the reason he was separated from you for a little while was that you might have him back for good—no longer as a slave, but better than a slave, as a dear brother. He is very dear to me but even dearer to you, both as a man and as a brother in the Lord. Philemon *15–16*

Philemon gives us a peek at how the early Christians tried to look at one another. One of the central characters of this letter was a runaway slave named Onesimus. Slaves who ran away were worse than outcasts. In fact, if Onesimus had been caught by someone other than Paul, he could have lost his life. Onesimus would have been hard pressed to find mercy anyplace other than in the Church. But God led him to a person who had not given up on him.

God does the same today when He leads people the world has given up on into our organizations. God doesn't look only at their sins and shortcomings. He looks at their God-given potential and calls us to help them realize it. People who run away from their responsibilities can have their lives changed by people who love them, take risks for them, and put the best construction on them.

Years ago, one class in our school had a nasty reputation. Teacher after teacher referred to the class as "them." My heart broke every time our teachers shook their heads over the trouble this class caused. The shaking of the head was done in a way that said, "What do you expect from kids like that?" No matter who stood up for this group, their words fell on deaf ears. "Don't confuse us with the facts. We've made up our minds. These are bad kids."

The teachers may have given up on these kids, but God hadn't. A decade later, this class has proven themselves to be bright, well-behaved, and faithful to the Lord and His people. What happened? They went to high schools where they had a new start. God turned them around. God surrounded them with people like St. Paul who showed them their errors, lovingly forgave them, and continued to encourage them.

As church workers, God has called us to minister to the Onesimuses of the world. The list of Onesimuses in the Bible is long, including the names of people like Abraham, Moses, David, Mary Magdalene, Peter, and Paul. God put the best construction on each of them.

Many years ago, a young man had a vicious screaming match with his father and angrily left home. After he was gone for two hours, his father called to request my prayers. While I was on the phone, I heard a knock at my office door. I put the father on hold and opened the door. It was the runaway boy. He said he needed someplace where people had confidence in him. His father was relieved.

Many youth and adults have been led to believe they don't measure up to society's expectations. We pray that God sends these people to us and that we may say to their spouses, children, or friends, "Perhaps the reason he was separated from you for a little while was that you might have him back for good." Grant this Lord to us all!

The Prayer: Almighty Creator, You love everyone. You sent Christ to die for my sins so You can put the best construction on my life. Help me to put the best construction on every person I meet. In Jesus' name and for His sake. Amen.

~68~

Jesus Loves Me, This I Know Because ...

"For God so loved the world that He gave His one and only Son, that whoever believes in Him shall not perish but have eternal life. For God did not send His Son into the world to condemn the world, but to save the world through Him." *John 3:16–17*

It's a Monday morning. I am at my desk going through the attendance cards filled out on Sunday. One member complained about the loudness of the organ. Another member complained about the length of the service. Still another member said the sermon contained "too much Gospel and not enough Law." Such Monday morning responses make me wonder whether God called me into the ministry or if I just ate a green apple.

I don't know for sure, but I imagine I'm not the only church worker who, in the face of criticism, wondered if they missed their calling. Most church workers take their work seriously and try to grow in their skills. They attend seminars and enroll in graduate programs designed to make them better servants. Sometimes their efforts aren't appreciated. People still question their methods and effectiveness.

Years ago, I learned what makes church workers effective. My wife and I loved to sleep in on Saturday mornings. We used to kid each other that if the Lord would return on a Saturday, we would be sleeping so soundly that we would miss it. Not this particular Saturday morning. We were awakened by our 2-year-old daughter singing in her room: "Geesus luv me, dis I know."

I was so excited. I told my wife that our daughter obviously was demonstrating potential for a great spiritual life. "She takes after me," I boasted. The child went on with her song. "Geesus, luv me dis I know, for my mommy told me so!" I was heartbroken. I moaned that this child knows absolutely nothing about the means of grace!

How silly I was. This child knew much about the grace of God that uses moms and dads to bring His Word into a child's life. God makes our ministries successful. He promised to do so and He always keeps His promise.

A church worker's effectiveness comes from God, who, through His Word, uses people with and without Ph.Ds or 100 continuing education units. He uses anyone with a faith willing to proclaim the Word in word and deed. Certainly there are times when we need to grow in our skills but never as a way to save our ministries. Our ministries are saved and empowered by Jesus, who will never leave us or forsake us.

When we get to heaven, I believe we will do a lot of singing. Perhaps we will sing "Jesus Loves Me." But maybe the words will change. In heaven, you will see people with whom you shared the Gospel. They might be singing: "Jesus loves me this I know, 'cause Pastor Schmidt (or Teacher Schulz, or DCE Armstrong, or Deaconess Young) told me so." Throughout eternity, our ears will be blessed with the sound of people singing praises to God because God used our ministry to proclaim the Word. So when the criticism comes, never lose sight of who really makes our work effective. Continue to go into the world and share Jesus.

The Prayer: Jesus, strengthen me when I face criticism. Help me keep it in balance, knowing You can accomplish anything in me. Point me toward the day I will be reunited with all believers in heaven. In Your name. Amen.

~69~

When We Succeed

> For I am the least of the apostles and do not even deserve to be called an apostle, because I persecuted the church of God. But by the grace of God I am what I am,, and His grace to me was not without effect. No, I worked harder than all of them—yet not I, but the grace of God that was with me. Whether, then, it was I or they, this is what we preach, and this is what you believed. *1 Corinthians 15:9–11*

There are times in ministry when everything works out well. The plan worked. Participants played out their roles perfectly. The applause and congratulations fill our ears. We take deep breaths of relief and thanksgiving and go home feeling satisfied and fulfilled. Some of us have these experiences every week! As much as that is a blessing, it is also a potential curse. Success and effusive adulation tempts us to believe that our sufficiency rests in ourselves. When that happens, envy, jealousy, conflict, and disaster are not far off.

The apostle Paul's way of handling success deserves study and emulation. Paul enjoyed incredible success. No one was responsible for planting more churches than he, which is a fact that looks even more awesome when you consider the "neighborhoods" in which he worked.

We know that God endowed Paul with every spiritual gift. Paul told us how he spoke in tongues better than any of the Christians in Corinth. He told us that he received visions and revelations from the Lord. He reported in 2 Corinthians 12 that God took him up to the "third heaven" where he heard inexpressible things, things that man is not permitted to tell. Paul had reason to brag, to lift himself up before others, but such was not his spirit. Paul took his direction from our Lord Jesus. When he spoke about his blessings and abilities, he said, "I will not boast about myself except about my weaknesses."

Instead of leaving behind stories about how Paul took Christianity to the world, he left behind stories of his weaknesses—weaknesses from which God always delivered him. In our humility, we don't want to be insincere. If we have worked hard toward a certain goal and it has been met, it would be wrong not to enjoy congratulations. We also let others know that God blessed our efforts for Jesus' sake. The people we serve grow from our example when we deal with our successes in this way. Those with whom we work grow in joy and in their desire to serve when we praise God for their ministries.

I once attended a three-day seminar designed to help pastors grow their churches with grace and dispatch. The pastor who hosted the seminar had watched God make his congregation one of the largest in the country. I learned a lot about programs, recruitment, and team ministries. What impressed me most, however, was the humble, thankful, grateful, quiet man who made it clear that God is responsible for the growth his congregation enjoyed.

May God give to all His church workers tremendous success. At the same time, may God give grace to deal with success in such a way as to give Him the glory.

The Prayer: Lord Jesus, I pray that You would continue to bless our churches with programs and ministries that grow and succeed. I also pray that You would allow us never to lose sight of the source of this sufficiency—You and You alone. Make and keep us humble servants, O Lord. In Your name, Jesus. Amen.

~70~

And Be Thankful

Let the peace of Christ rule in your hearts, since as members of one body you were called to peace. And be thankful. *Colossians 3:15*

Generations of church workers have lifted up our Lord's words in Matthew 28:19: "Therefore go and make disciples of all nations, baptizing them in the name of the Father and of the Son and of the Holy Spirit." These words give the church her marching orders. But these words, on their own, don't provide us with the reason to go. Those words come in the preceding verse. "All authority in heaven and on earth has been given to Me." Church workers cling to these words to remain strong in faith and service.

In essence, these words say that Jesus is the boss of the universe, and this boss loves us passionately. Our boss has the authority to prevent darkness from overtaking the Light that we proclaim daily. It may get cloudy every now and then, but the One who has all authority will maintain His bright light.

Our boss has authority to drive out illness and death. He can heal people temporally and eternally. However He chooses to heal us, we will be in better shape than we were before we became ill. Our boss has authority to take something as evil as Egypt's oppression of Israel and turn it into an occasion for deliverance, comfort, and strength. Our boss has the desire and the ability to proclaim His lifesaving Word through us.

Because our beloved boss has all authority, an authority He uses to bless us, one phrase characterizes our ministries: Thank You. Thank You, Lord, first for our salvation. Thank You for calling us into Your service and numbering us among all who have served You. Thank You for assuring us that there isn't a problem that You can't solve. Thank You for being the same, yesterday, today, and forever so we don't have to wonder if You will run out of patience or power. Thank You, Lord, for the people we serve—souls and heels alike. Thank You, Lord, for the people we will serve in the future. Thank You, Lord, for our brothers and sisters in Christ. And Lord, please allow us to let the thanks we feel in our hearts be visible in our smiles. You have all authority in heaven and on earth, and for that, Lord, please accept our eternal thanks.

The Prayer: Dear Jesus, thank You for sending me into the world to make disciples. I especially thank You for using Your authority to help me in this task. Make me a confident, excited, enthusiastic, and thankful servant to Your glory and to the benefit of the world. In Your blessed name I pray, Jesus. Amen.